The Pegasus Story
A history of a vintage British computer

Simon Lavington

Science Museum

British Library Cataloguing-in-Publication Data
A catalogue record for this publication is available from the British Library

Set in Postscript Monotype Plantin by Jerry Fowler
Printed in Great Britain by the Cromwell Press
Cover artwork by Jerry Fowler

ISBN 1 900747 40 5

Science Museum, Exhibition Road, London SW7 2DD
http://www.nmsi.ac.uk

Contents

Bibliography and references

For a general account of information technology developments worldwide from the 1840s (Babbage) to the World Wide Web (1990s), see: M Campbell-Kelly and W Asprey, *Computer: a history of the information machine*. Basic Books, New York, 1996.

For descriptions of pioneering stored-program computers worldwide, mostly written by the pioneers themselves, see: N Metropolis, J Howlett and G-C Rota (editors), *A History of Computing in the Twentieth Century*. Academic Press, 1980.

Refer also to various articles in back numbers of the IEEE journal *Annals of the History of Computing*.

For an account of the main UK pioneering computers, see: S H Lavington, *Early British Computers*. Manchester University Press, 1980.

For a contemporary account of many British projects, see: B V Bowden, *Faster than Thought: a symposium on digital computing machines*. Pitman, 1953.

A list of 70 references to Pegasus and to Pegasus-related historical computers, accompanied by additional notes on the text of this booklet, will be found at:

http://cswww.essex.ac.uk/Pegasus/

Acknowledgements

Many computer pioneers and historical experts have helped with the writing of this booklet. Special thanks are due to Prof. John Bennett, Chris Burton, Harry Carpenter, Laurence Clarke, John Crawley, Hugh Devonald, Elizabeth Elliott, George Felton, Sir John Fairclough, Sebastian de Ferranti, Peter Hall, Ed Hersom, Len Hewitt, Peter Holland, Harry Johnson, Ian Merry, Colin Merton, Derek Milledge, Hugh Ross, Dag Spicer, Andrew St Johnston and Prof. John Wilson. Notwithstanding their willing help, the author takes final responsibility for the text. It is with much sadness that we record the deaths in May 2000 of Prof. Bill Elliott, after a long illness, and in July 2000 of Derek Milledge.

Links

A Pegasus simulator, which runs on a PC, may be accessed at:

ftp://ftp.cs.man.ac.uk/pub/CCS-Archive/simulators/Pegasus

Another useful link is to the Computer Conservation Society, whose members restored and maintain the Pegasus on display in the Science Museum:

http://www.cs.man.ac.uk/CCS/

Foreword

The history of post-war British computing is a tale largely untold. The latter-day might of the United States tends to overshadow the pioneering achievements of British computer designers, and in our salutes to those who ultimately triumphed we tend to forget that the fledgling world of post-war computing was rich in the rivalry of equals.

The history of modern computing is remarkable in that the earliest electronic computers are still within the span of living memory. It is doubly important, therefore, that these histories are captured while first-hand accounts are still possible, so that our perceptions can be tethered to the experiences of those involved at the time. The material captured in this book reflects not only Simon Lavington's deep knowledge of the period and his command of contemporary computing technologies, but is also informed by comments and feedback from many of those associated with the events recounted. Future historians, not so blessed by access to the surviving players, will construct their own histories. This tale is ours.

The Science Museum has a special relationship with Pegasus. The twenty-fifth Pegasus to be built, completed in 1959, resides in the Museum's collections, and this book marks its return to public display. Pegasus No. 25, a vacuum-tube machine, has been restored to working order through the voluntary efforts of the Computer Conservation Society, a specialist group jointly founded in 1989 by the British Computer Society and the Science Museum. It is the only surviving working Pegasus, and among the very few working, contemporary vacuum-tube machines anywhere. The fact that this machine was successfully restored to working order is a tribute to the durability of its design and construction, as well as to the dedicated efforts of its restorers.

Powered up, in full 'flight', Pegasus is a sight to behold. To witness the machine in operation is to be reminded of a bygone age when the future impact of computers was barely foreseen. Simon Lavington's *Pegasus Story* is a splendid companion to the machine itself and an invaluable record of a distinguished chapter in British computing history.

Doron Swade
Assistant Director and Head of Collections
Science Museum, London

Guide to early computer technology

Memory systems

Electronic storage devices were mostly of three forms: magnetic drums, delay lines, or electrostatic storage. *Magnetic drums* were similar to modern hard disks, in that binary digits were recorded on a magnetically-coated surface. Most drums had a fixed read/write head for every information track on the drum's surface. In *delay line storage* systems, electronic pulses representing binary information were converted into ultrasonic sound pulses, transmitted through a medium such as *mercury* or *nickel*, re-converted into electrical pulses, and then recirculated as sound pulses. The sound pulses travel through the medium much more slowly than electronic pulses travel along a piece of wire. Thus, a computer operating at electronic speeds could effectively store information for a time in the medium. In *electrostatic storage* systems, binary information was stored as electrostatic charge patterns on the phosphor inner coating of a glass cathode ray tube (*CRT*). Since the charge leaks away, special electronic means had to be devised for refreshing the pattern of stored charge. The *Williams Tube* (or *Williams/Kilburn Tube*) was the main example of electrostatic storage in the early days of computers.

Computing circuits

Most early computers used *thermionic valves* (*vacuum tubes*) instead of transistors or silicon chips. Valves were the basic electronic components used for switching and amplifying binary signals, and hence for carrying out the logical, arithmetic and control functions inside the computer. *Triodes* and *pentodes* were the names of two types of valve.

Input/output equipment

Programmers of early electronic computers prepared their programs and data either on *punched paper tape* or on *punched cards*. Binary information was represented by the presence or absence of holes punched in specific places on the tape or card. An electronic input device attached to the computer was able to 'read' the information which had been punched. Output, i.e. results, produced by the computer could be automatically punched on tape or cards by an electronic output device. Alternatively, or additionally, a printer was attached to the computer.

1 What is Pegasus?

Figure 1.1 In the 1950s, computers were large and interesting pieces of scientific apparatus with plenty of switches and lights. Pegasus was important because it was comparatively easy to use, easy to manufacture in quantity and very reliable. Some of Pegasus' ideas on ease of use have had a strong influence on subsequent computer design. The origins of the Pegasus project are complicated, involving a series of contracts from the National Research Development Corporation to two UK companies, starting in 1951 at a time when only a dozen computers were in operation worldwide.

Pegasus is the name of a British-designed computer produced by the UK company Ferranti Ltd. The first Pegasus went into service in March 1956, at a time when all of the computers then in use in the UK were designed and built in Britain. To understand why Pegasus was an interesting landmark in the development of information processing, we have to turn back the clock to the days before the Internet, before the personal computer, before the supercomputer – in fact to the days when even the word 'computer' had a different meaning. Prior to 1945, the word 'computer' meant only one thing: a clerk equipped with a hand calculating machine who would 'compute' the standard calculations required for wages, aircraft design, gunnery (ballistics) tables, and so on. To most people, 'computing' was essentially a numeric activity. The thought that a computing device might one day be used for non-numeric information, such as in databases and word processors, was simply unimaginable.

By the end of 1949 there were probably only four prototype, automatic, electronic computing machines which had come into hesitant operation anywhere in the world. These included two in the UK (at the universities of Cambridge and Manchester), one in the USA (at the Eckert-Mauchley Computer Corporation) and one in Australia (at the Commonwealth Scientific and Industrial Research Organisation). By the middle of 1951, at which time the research that led to Pegasus was getting under way, the number of computers in operation worldwide had risen to about a dozen. As with the very early days of motor cars, these dozen pioneering machines were all subtly different. They were, so to speak, the hand-crafted test-beds for a rich variety of designs and technologies. Their designers were exploring the digital space, without the benefit of market feedback.

Into this space stepped Pegasus. With a name like Pegasus, images of a winged stallion spring to mind. Actually, Pegasus was more of a sweet-tempered workhorse than a highly-strung thoroughbred. Its designers had had the opportunity to observe some of the difficulties in using the earliest computers. They undertook to make Pegasus much more user-friendly. Although hidden from view inside a silicon chip, remnants of the ideas on ease of use formulated for Pegasus are found in most modern computers.

The notion of a user-friendly computer in the mid-1950s is one that may now be hard for us to understand. We have to think switches and lamps,

Figure 1.2 The sixth Pegasus computer to be built was delivered to Vickers-Armstrong (Aircraft) Ltd at Weybridge, south-west of London, in May 1957. It was used during the next dozen years for design calculations for aircraft such as the VC-10, BAC 1-11 and Concorde. The photograph shows the Pegasus input/output equipment on the table-tops in the foreground, to the left and right of the operator. The main computer is housed in the tall cabinets that look rather like a three-bay wardrobe. Not shown in the picture are two more cabinets housing the power supplies, and the remotely-located motor–alternator machinery which connected those cabinets to the mains electricity supply. (Photo courtesy of Ferranti archive and ICL. Photo supplied by Mrs Judith Milledge.)

rather than keyboards and screens; we have to think binary digits rather than clickable icons. More crucially, we have to think back to a time when there was no formal training in information technology or computer science and where, as happened with Pegasus, an enthusiastic amateur could have an idea that contributed significantly to the functional capabilities of Pegasus and its successors.

Pegasus was a team effort, in the sense that the dedication and skills of perhaps 35 people contributed, over a period of about five years, to the hardware and software of the final Pegasus product. Many of the team members had spent the war years working under extreme pressure on weapons-related technologies such as radar. The wartime culture of urgency and innovation spilled over into post-war projects well into the 1950s. The effect of external management and marketing decisions on the human dynamics of this team was traumatic for them, and is fascinating to us. As things turned out, the story did have a happy ending. Pegasus computers enjoyed long and successful careers, during which their innovative features proved beneficial. A total of 40 Pegasus machines were built, of which three were exported (to Canada, Germany and Sweden). Ferranti Ltd delivered the last Pegasus in October 1962. Pegasus computers were put to work in a variety of engineering companies, banks, universities and research establishments. For most of these organisations and their staff, Pegasus was their first computer and therefore the herald of a new age.

Because of its wide availability at an interesting period in the growth of the computer industry, Pegasus became something of a personal benchmark for many UK computer professionals. This fact, coupled with Pegasus' novel internal design, makes it an important artefact in the history of the information revolution in Britain. It is indeed fortunate that the twenty-fifth Pegasus machine to be built is still in working order at the time of writing and on display in the Science Museum, London.

Figure 1.3 A feature of Pegasus is its modular construction, using robust plug-in electronic packages. In this 1956 photograph an engineer has opened one of the computer's cabinets and is in the process of extracting a package which is the size of a paperback book. Originally called the Ferranti Packaged Computer, the project's name was changed to the similarly-sounding 'Ferranti Pegasus Computer' by the company's sales staff. Internally, the Pegasus logical structure embodied an innovative 'general register set' architecture which is still used in many modern computers. (Photo courtesy of Ferranti archive and ICL.)

2 The birth of Pegasus

2.1 Prelude: computer developments in the USA and UK, 1945–51

The modern computer or, more technically, the universal stored-program digital computer, was an outgrowth of several strands of research and development in the period up to 1950. Most of the early research took place in the USA and Britain, accelerated by the technical challenges of the Second World War. In the light of hindsight we can now distinguish theoretical, technical and entrepreneurial strands in a rich tapestry of innovation that forms the backdrop to the birth of the modern computer. In the late 1940s, individual pioneers were less certain about the outcome of their labours.

The phrase 'stored-program computer' implies the ability of a machine to hold both instructions and data in an internal read/write memory. The provision of a cost-effective main memory, or store, was the principal engineering problem facing all designers of early stored-program computers (see Figure 2.1). Summarising the worldwide computer scene during 1949, Nathaniel Rochester (of IBM) wrote in the premier US electronics journal of the time: 'The most difficult problem in the construction of large-scale digital computers continues to be the question of how to build a memory, and the few papers written do not reflect the greatness of the effort which is being exerted.'

The developments which led to Pegasus covered the period 1946–56, being a combination of expertise accumulated by two British companies, Elliott Brothers (London) Ltd and Ferranti Ltd, actively encouraged by the UK's National Research Development Corporation (NRDC). The NRDC was founded in July 1949, after public concern that British ideas were being exploited abroad to the eventual disadvantage of British industry. One of the first tasks of the NRDC was to take over from the Ministry of Supply certain patents on computer storage (i.e. memory) technology that had resulted from research at the University of Manchester.

Well-placed figures in the UK scientific establishment, including Professor Douglas Hartree of Cambridge University, Professor Max Newman of Manchester University and Sir Ben Lockspeiser, Chief Scientist at the Ministry of Supply, had foreseen the importance of computers. It is therefore not surprising that the NRDC quickly set up an Advisory Panel on

Figure 2.1 In the late 1940s the main practical problem in building electronic digital computers was to devise suitable storage, or memory, technologies. Three of the devices employed are shown in the photograph. At the top is a cathode ray tube (CRT) used for electrostatic storage. In the centre is a twin steel tube filled with mercury, giving a form of delay-line storage. To the right is another form of delay-line storage based on a coil of nickel wire. Devices similar to these three could each store approximately one thousand binary digits ('bits'). For comparison, in the foreground is a modern silicon memory chip which can store many millions of bits. (Photo courtesy of the Department of Computer Science, University of Manchester.)

Electronic Computers. This Panel held but one meeting, on 14 December 1949, attended by all the major UK electronics and office machinery companies of the time. Although this initiative failed to produce a coordinated national effort, the meeting did convince NRDC that it should actively encourage individual companies to enter the computer field. One of the outcomes was a study contract with Elliott's Borehamwood Research Laboratory. Work on the NRDC contract began in earnest in June 1951; this marked the start of focused R&D which eventually led to the birth of Pegasus. Mid-1951 is therefore a good point at which to review the state of other pioneering computer projects in the USA and Britain.

2.1.1 The US scene in 1951

During and immediately after the Second World War, several large automatic computing projects were undertaken in the USA. At the start of this period, computing machines depended upon electro-mechanical, rather than electronic, computational equipment and generally held their list of instructions (their 'program') externally on some form of punched paper tape or punched card. The outcome of this strand of development was IBM's Selective Sequence Electronic Calculator (SSEC), first working early in 1948. The SSEC, nick-named 'Poppa' on account of its physical size, contained 23,000 electro-mechanical relays and 13,000 thermionic valves (vacuum tubes). With the advance of electronic circuit techniques, the speed – and to some extent the generality – of computing machines increased dramatically during the 1940s. This is exemplified by the US army's

Electronic Numerical Integrator and Computer (ENIAC), first working in the autumn of 1945. ENIAC contained 18,000 thermionic valves and 1500 electro-mechanical relays, and weighed over 30 tonnes. It was primarily intended for use in ballistics computing for gunnery tables, but was put to other uses in the years following its inauguration. As an illustration of ENIAC's usefulness, a skilled person with a mechanical desk calculator could compute a 60-second trajectory of a projectile in about 20 hours. A special electro-mechanical device called a differential analyser could do the same calculations with rather less accuracy in 15 minutes. ENIAC, once set up, required only 30 seconds to perform the same calculation accurately.

Although the SSEC and ENIAC were technological masterpieces, neither machine was what we would now class as a true stored-program computer. However, the substantial effort surrounding the huge ENIAC project led directly to a seminal document known as the EDVAC Report in June 1945. This report was the first widely-available discussion of how the stored-program concept might be implemented. This ENIAC and EDVAC activity had, by 1951, spawned four working stored-program computers in the USA and several more in part-completion. To this list should be added other projects which grew out of non-ENIAC military contracts. A total of six US computers had actually run their first program by mid-1951, though only the five shown in Table 2.1 were still operational.

2.1.2 *The British scene in 1951*

Some historians now believe that both the theoretical and practical principles of a universal stored-program computer may have been familiar to the British mathematicians Dr Alan Turing and Professor Max Newman by the end of the Second World War. This was partly because of their own pre-war mathematical research and partly as a result of their wartime code-breaking activity at Bletchley Park in Buckinghamshire. Bletchley Park was the Government Code and Cypher School. A major electronic aid to code-breaking at Bletchley Park was the series of Colossus electronic machines, the first of which contained 1500 thermionic valves and began useful decryption work in December 1943. Ten enlarged Colossus Mark II machines, each containing 2500 valves, came into operation at Bletchley Park from June 1944. Although able to perform high-speed logical and conditional branching operations on parallel bit-streams, Colossus was certainly not a stored-program computer. Furthermore, strict secrecy ensured that none of the Colossus know-how was readily available in 1951. Nevertheless, a few UK computer projects, such as the Ministry of Supply's

MOSAIC and the National Physical Laboratory's Pilot ACE, may have benefited from indirect knowledge of Bletchley Park's digital design activity.

Apart from government establishments, much of the initial British stored-program activity was concentrated in three places: Cambridge University, Manchester University and the National Physical Laboratory (NPL). Other early British projects existed at London University (at Birkbeck College and Imperial College). By mid-1951, five stored-program computers were working in the UK (see Table 2.1). All five British projects were less

Computer	Date first delivered	Organisation working	Memory technology
EDSAC	May. 1949	Cambridge University, UK	Mercury delay lines
Mark I	Oct. 1949	(a) Manchester University, UK	CRT (Williams/Kilburn)
CSIRAC	Nov. 1949	(b) CSIRO, Australia	Mercury delay lines
Pilot ACE	May. 1950	National Physical Labs, UK	Mercury delay lines
SWAC	Aug. 1950	National Bureau of Standards, USA	CRT (Williams/Kilburn)
Whirlwind	Nov. 1950	MIT, USA	CRT (special)
ERA 1101	Dec. 1950	Engineering Research Assoc., USA	Magnetic drum
Ferranti Mark I	Feb. 1951	Ferranti Ltd, UK	CRT (Williams/Kilburn)
LEO	Feb. 1951	(c) J Lyons & Co., UK	Mercury delay lines
UNIVAC	Mar. 1951	Eckert-Mauchly Corp., USA	Mercury delay lines
SEAC	May. 1951	National Bureau of Standards, USA	Mercury delay lines

Table 2.1 Stored-program computers in operation worldwide in June 1951, at a time when the R&D that led to Pegasus was just starting. The table gives the approximate date when each computer first ran a program, the originating organisation and the technology used for the main memory. (The Pegasus memory technology differed from all of those shown.) It is fair to say that many of the machines were prototypes and development continued after the date shown.

Notes

(a) The Manchester University Mark I, sometimes called MADM, was the enlarged version of the Small-Scale Experimental Machine (SSEM, or 'baby'). On 21 June 1948 the SSEM was the first computer in the world to demonstrate convincingly the stored-program principle.

(b) CSIRAC was designed by Trevor Pearcey and colleagues at the Commonwealth Scientific & Industrial Research Centre's Radiophysics Division, Sydney.

(c) LEO, or Lyons Electronic Office, was a development of the Cambridge EDSAC computer but with larger memory and multiple higher-speed input/output channels. At the time, LEO was unique: it demonstrated the possibilities of business information processing years ahead of the application of computers to comparable UK commercial organisations.

Figure 2.2 Some of the Borehamwood designers who worked on government contracts for naval anti-aircraft fire-control systems were photographed in 1948 or 1949, at a project presentation to visiting US naval personnel. The fire-control contracts involved innovative digital computer technology and packaged electronic circuitry which later influenced what became the Pegasus project. John Coales, seen at the front of the photograph, established the Borehamwood Research Laboratory in 1946. (Photo courtesy of Ed Hersom.)

ambitious than contemporary US endeavours. Size apart, closer study of the internal design of all 11 computers in the table reveals plenty of differences as well as plenty of similarities. This was the era of exploration.

2.2 Borehamwood, the NRDC and Pegasus predecessors

Any engineer who was involved with the design of Pegasus or its local predecessors would have been aware of the existence, though not necessarily the details, of most of the 11 pioneering computers listed in Table 2.1. However, the field was still speculative and the strengths and weaknesses of each pioneering design were not yet generally apparent. In industry and commerce, stored-program computers were regarded, at best, as of marginal scientific interest. In the UK, the punched-card and office equipment manufacturers such as the British Tabulating Machine Company (BTM) were slow to get involved.

The National Research Development Corporation (NRDC) was rather more ambitious. The Corporation was well aware that Ferranti Ltd was, by 1950, collaborating with Manchester University on what promised to be a powerful, but comparatively expensive, commercially-available computer. Indeed, later, in October 1951, NRDC gave considerable financial help to Ferranti to produce four of the large Ferranti Mark I Star computers. NRDC also believed that there was a need for cheaper, medium-scale computers and that the Borehamwood Research Laboratories of Elliott Brothers Ltd was the place to start.

We shall see later that, although NRDC was the midwife, Pegasus did not have a particularly easy birth. The four-year gestation period involved a transfer of people and know-how between two companies, starting at Elliott's Borehamwood Research Laboratories and ending at Ferranti's London Computer Centre. As the story unfolds, it may be helpful to visualise the related computer design and prototyping activity as a time-chart (see Figure 2.3). To set all this in context, we first need to make a small digression and explain why, in the first place, Borehamwood attracted the attention of NRDC.

2.2.1 Borehamwood

Immediately after the end of the Second World War, the Admiralty approached several British companies with a proposal to set up a research laboratory to develop a new anti-aircraft fire-control and radar system for the navy. The project required that ship-borne radar lock on to a target at

Figure 2.3 Computer design activity at Elliott Brothers Ltd (Borehamwood) and Ferranti Ltd, surrounding the birth of the first Pegasus.

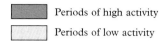

Periods of high activity

Periods of low activity

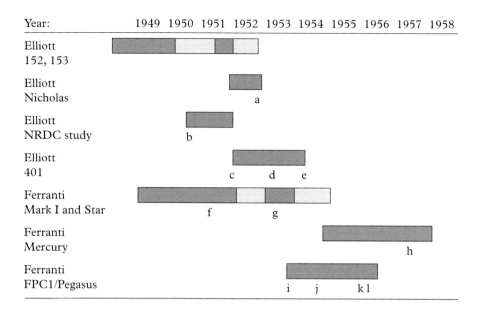

Notes on significant dates

a Nicholas first runs a program, December 1952.
b NRDC contract to Elliott Bros., Borehamwood, dated September 1950.
c NRDC contract to Elliott Bros., Borehamwood, dated April 1952.
d The Elliott/NRDC 401 first runs a program, March 1953.
e The Elliott/NRDC 401 handed over to Rothamsted, March 1954.
f First Ferranti Mark I delivered, Feb. 1951; last one delivered 1952.
g First Ferranti Mark I Star delivered, 1953; last one delivered 1957.
h First Ferranti Mercury delivered, Aug. 1957; last one delivered May 1961.
i NRDC contract to Ferranti, dated November 1953.
j NRDC contract to Ferranti, dated December 1954.
k Ferranti Pegasus first runs a program, October 1955.
l Ferranti Pegasus first used by external customers at the London Computer Centre, April 1956.

about eight miles and then track it and supply aiming information to a ship's guns. The company finally chosen for the task was Elliott Brothers Ltd, producers of most of the fire-control predictors for naval surface gunnery during the war. John Coales, who had been responsible for naval gunnery radar since 1939, was given the job of starting a new Elliott Brothers'

Figure 2.4 W S (Bill) Elliott (1917–2000). After war service developing radar systems, Bill joined the Borehamwood Research Laboratories of Elliott Brothers (London) Ltd in 1947. There he led the Computing Division and oversaw the design and development of the Elliott/NRDC 401 computer. Bill Elliott moved to Ferranti Ltd in 1953, where he led the team that designed the Pegasus computer. He joined IBM in 1956, to organise the founding of IBM's UK Laboratories at Hursley. In 1966 he became Professor of Computing at Imperial College, London. The photograph shows Professor Elliott in 1993 at the Science Museum, with the original drum store from the 401 computer.

Research Laboratory at Borehamwood in Hertfordshire. By October 1946, work had started at Borehamwood on the MRS4 (later MRS5) project, an automatic, digital, medium-range anti-aircraft fire-control system. The total staff at Borehamwood had expanded to over 400 by 1950 – an extraordinary rate of growth. Within Borehamwood there was a Computing Division managed by W S (Bill) Elliott – no relation of the company's founders (Figure 2.4). This Computing Division was responsible for a section of the MRS5 project known as the type 152 digital fire-control computer (Figure 2.5) which used a novel printed-circuit packaged technology. The electronics of the 152 were designed by a team led by Harry Carpenter, which included Andrew St Johnston and contribution from Charles Owen.

The Pegasus story starts in 1950, when Lord Halsbury, the Managing Director of NRDC, had the vision of a medium-priced computer which would combine the Williams Tube electrostatic CRT storage (for which NRDC administered the patents) with the packaged circuit technology then under development at Borehamwood. To modern eyes, the NRDC vision seems clear: electrostatic storage would provide a low cost-per-bit memory; the packaged technology offered manufacturing modularity and ease of maintenance; the whole project would serve to propel an innovative UK electronics team (at Borehamwood) into an important but unfilled sector of a growing market. From NRDC's viewpoint, the whole Borehamwood exercise would nicely complement the efforts of Ferranti Ltd, who were just beginning to sell high-performance computers at the top end of the market.

By the time the first NRDC contract was placed with Borehamwood in September 1950, this laboratory was actually moving away from the earlier form of anticipation-pulse Williams/Kilburn tube storage because of reliability problems. The NRDC contract provided a spur to Borehamwood's search for an alternative memory technology. Knowing that nickel variable delay lines had been employed for pulse storage in the USA in 1950, for NAVAR and similar radar-based air navigational systems, Bill Elliott's group realised that nickel delay lines could also be used for computer memory. An explanation of how a piece of nickel wire can be used to store digital information is given in Chapter 3. It is probable that Borehamwood was attracted to the idea because nickel lines were cheaper per bit and more robust than mercury delay lines. Nickel lines were also more reliable and more robust than CRT electrostatic storage, but more expensive per bit.

Thus it was that the first tangible Borehamwood output of the NRDC packaged circuitry contract was a proof-of-concept demonstrator called

Figure 2.5 Part of the type 152 special-purpose, real-time, computer developed between 1947 and 1950 at the Borehamwood Research Laboratories of Elliott Brothers (London) Ltd. The 152 was intended for naval gunnery control. It executed several instruction streams in parallel from an electrostatic read-only memory (ROM). The computer used sub-miniature thermionic valves mounted on novel glass printed-circuit boards or 'packages'. The National Research Development Corporation (NRDC) later placed contracts with Borehamwood to apply the company's expertise in packaged circuit technology to general-purpose computers. Packaged circuits were to become a feature of the Pegasus design. (Photo courtesy of S L H Clarke.)

SNARK – short nickel line accumulating register calculator – demonstrated at the Physical Society's Exhibition in London early in 1952. Independently of the NRDC contract, nickel delay lines were also used successfully at Borehamwood in an in-house stored-program computer called Nicholas (see Figure 2.6), which first ran a program in December 1952 – but that's another story. Nicholas was designed by Charles Owen. A couple of years later, experience with Nicholas contributed to the design of Pegasus.

Pleased with the SNARK demonstrator, NRDC placed a follow-on contract with Borehamwood in April 1952 for the construction of a fully operational, low-cost stored-program computer. Under Bill Elliott, Andrew St Johnston led the detailed design team, which included Laurence Clarke, Hugh Devonald, Norman Muchmore and Berwick Stallworthy. The internal NRDC job number for the project was 401. Thus, the Elliott/NRDC 401 computer was born (see Figure 2.7). At first the intention was to use nickel delay lines for the entire memory of the 401 computer. In the end, nickel delay lines were only used for central registers. The main memory was a magnetic disk, designed by Chris Phillips, because the disk provided the desired storage

Figure 2.6 Nicholas, a general-purpose computer built in 1952 for in-house problem-solving in the Theory Laboratory at Borehamwood. Nicholas was designed by Charles Owen in about four weeks, while he was off work at home recovering from mumps. It used nickel delay-line storage units, with a total capacity of 1024 words (4 kbytes). On the programming side, George Felton was responsible for the system software (i.e. standard library subroutines). Although appearing rather home-made, Nicholas gave valuable service from 1952 to 1958. Experience with Nicholas contributed later to the design of Pegasus. (Photo courtesy of S L H Clarke.)

capacity at lower cost than an all-nickel memory. This had consequences for the 401's performance, since the disk was a sequential memory, whose revolution-time (latency) could significantly slow down some accesses to code and data. To help reduce delays, the 401's instruction set was based on a so-called one-plus-one (1+1) address format, where the location of the next instruction was specified in the present instruction. With knowledge of the disk's timing, programmers were able to place their instructions optimally on disk so as to achieve faster overall run-times. This was the

Figure 2.7 The Elliott/NRDC 401 computer, designed and built at Borehamwood under a contract from the National Research Development Corporation (NRDC). The plug-in electronic circuit packages in the centre three bays give the appearance of books in a bookcase. The magnetic drum (or disk) memory is housed in the upper right-hand compartment. The 401 computer, first working in 1953, was handed over to the Rothamsted Agricultural Experimental Station in 1954, where it was in use until 1965. (Photo courtesy of S L H Clarke.)

technique known as optimum programming, also called minimum-latency coding. The 401's electronic circuits in the arithmetic unit were based on re-designed Elliott 152 packages mounted on Paxolin ('plastic') instead of glass, using dual-triode thermionic valves instead of sub-miniature pentode valves.

2.2.2 The 401 computer and staff movements

The Elliott/NRDC 401 computer first ran a program in March 1953. It was exhibited at the Physical Society Exhibition in London from 3 to 8 April, running demonstration programs written by an NRDC consultant called Christopher Strachey – of whom more later. This is believed to have been the first time (possibly in the world) that a general-purpose stored-program computer was put on public display at an exhibition site. After the exhibition, the 401 was moved back to Borehamwood and then, in June 1953, to Cambridge University for further trials. At Cambridge Christopher Strachey, Harry Carpenter and others implemented a number of improvements. In March 1954, the NRDC handed the 401 over to the Rothamsted Agricultural Experimental Station in Hertfordshire, now the Institute of Arable Crops Research, where it gave splendid service until being retired on 30 July 1965. The 401 was eventually presented to the Science Museum in London, where, at the time of writing, it is being restored to working order by the Computer Conservation Society.

The movement of the 401 away from Borehamwood was not the only departure. The period 1952–53 saw some complex management changes at Elliott Brothers Ltd that cannot easily be described here. The practical consequences were that by the end of 1952 John Coales (Head of the Borehamwood Laboratories) had resigned, closely followed by Bill Elliott (Head of the Computing Division at Borehamwood). Their resignations did not take effect until May 1953, when they both moved to Cambridge. Towards the end of 1953 Bill Elliott joined Ferranti Ltd, and was followed by other Borehamwood personnel such as Charles Owen and Hugh Devonald. George Felton, who had led the program development for the Elliott Nicholas computer, also moved to Ferranti in 1954 to join the team.

By November 1953 NRDC had decided to transfer its hopes for the production of a medium-scale, low-cost packaged computer to a team at Ferranti Ltd headed by Bill Elliott. The new NRDC contract first referred to the machine as the Ferranti Packaged Computer, number 1 (FPC1). In mid-1954 the Ferranti Sales Department re-named the machine Pegasus, and the change of name was officially adopted in January 1955. The nomenclature set a fashion for astronomy and mythology within the Ferranti company, which produced machines such as Mercury, Perseus, Sirius, Orion, Atlas and Argus computers in the late 1950s and early 1960s. The relationship of some of these later computers to Pegasus is discussed in Chapter 5.

Back at Borehamwood, Andrew St Johnston took over the leadership of a reorganised Elliott Computing Division, which went on to produce the Elliott 402 and 405 computers and other successful machines. Other projects, such as the 800 series (1958 onwards) and the 500 series followed. By 1968 the main computer-manufacturing interests of Elliott Brothers had been subsumed in a series of company amalgamations which produced International Computers Ltd (ICL), as mentioned in Chapter 5.

To continue the Pegasus story, NRDC's shift of focus from Elliott Brothers Ltd to Ferranti Ltd is illustrated in the time-chart of Figure 2.3. This shows how there was an accumulation of experience spread across two companies which, by one means or another, contributed to the final production Pegasus. Prior to 1954, Ferranti Ltd operated at the higher-performance end of the computer business, as a result of fruitful links with Manchester University dating from 1948. Collaboration with the University produced the

Ferranti Mark I, Mark I Star and (later) the Mercury and Atlas computers. Then, from 1954 onwards, this Manchester-based high-performance culture found itself co-existing with a London-based mid-range culture imported by Bill Elliott and colleagues. We return to this subject in Chapter 4.

2.3 Christopher Strachey and Ferranti Ltd

This is the moment to introduce Christopher Strachey into the Pegasus story (Figure 2.8). Strachey made notable contributions to several areas of computer science until his untimely death in 1975 at the age of 59. He became a consultant to NRDC in 1952 and, in 1953, wrote demonstration programs for the NRDC/Elliott 401 computer.

In 1953–54 Strachey, on request, became involved in the specification of the NRDC follow-on contract, awarded to Ferranti Ltd, for a re-designed and improved packaged computer. In the light of hindsight, we can see that Strachey was well placed to make a major contribution to the design of what became the influential Pegasus product. Firstly, he was an independently minded consultant with first-hand experience of programming three other computers. Secondly, he was able, through his wartime work for an electronics company, to bridge the conceptual gap between mathematicians and engineers or, as we might say today, between software and hardware. Thirdly, his later research into the theory of programming languages, particularly denotational semantics, testifies to his ability to generalise and formalise.

Strachey's contribution to Pegasus lay in the realm of what we would now call systems architecture: principally the instruction set, the address-generation mechanisms and the logical memory organisation. With respect to the Pegasus instruction set, Strachey focused especially on what he called the 'red tape' orders, which included control-transfers (jump, or branch, instructions), data transfers between levels of physical storage, and how structured data such as large arrays were to be accessed (see Chapter 3).

Strachey's aim was to produce a computer that was easier to program than existing machines of the early 1950s. An idea of his motivation may be gained from the following quote from a 1956 scientific paper describing Pegasus, in which index registers are given their original name of B-lines: 'In the Manchester University computer the B-lines serve two very valuable but distinct purposes: they allow order modification and rudimentary arithmetic (such as counting) to be done without disturbing the accumulator. It was felt that fuller arithmetic and logical facilities on these

Figure 2.8 Christopher Strachey (1916–75). In 1951, while working as a schoolteacher, Strachey was given the opportunity to write programs for both the NPL Pilot ACE and the Ferranti Mark I computers. Such was his skill at programming that he was offered a job at NRDC. In the period 1952–59 Strachey worked for NRDC on applications programming, low-level software and computer design. In 1953 he suggested improvements to the logical design of the 401 and, in the period 1954–55 made significant contributions to the design of Pegasus. After NRDC, Strachey moved to Cambridge University and then, from 1965, to Oxford where he carried out research in the theory of programming languages. (Photo courtesy of Barbara Halpern and Martin Campbell-Kelly.)

B-lines would have been extremely valuable. The seven accumulators in Pegasus, used for modification and arithmetic, are a development of the B-line concept.' Furthermore, we may quote from Bernard Swann, the Ferranti Sales Director of the time, who states that, 'Optimum programming was to be avoided because it tended to become a time-wasting intellectual hobby of programmers.' One might add that optimum programming also tended to make the intensive use of subroutines more difficult.

The result of these sentiments is to be seen in the powerful, straightforward Pegasus instruction set described in the next chapter. In contrast, the 401's 32-bit instruction format had what would nowadays be considered somewhat of the flavour of a microprogram instruction. The 401 programmer was obliged to work out entries for four three-bit fields in each instruction which specified function and control information, whereas the coding for the single Pegasus op.code field was more immediately understandable to first-time programmers. (The op.code, or 'operation code' field specifies the function, e.g. add, subtract, etc. being performed by an instruction.) Furthermore, the 401's ten-bit next-instruction address field was omitted from Pegasus, since Pegasus executed instructions from a fast, random-access (or immediate-access) memory. Thus, the location of each Pegasus instruction had no bearing on the speed of execution. In one respect Pegasus was superficially similar to the 401 because the machines had the same digit period. However, the 401's packaged circuits were re-designed for Pegasus in respect of logical function, component values and physical connectors, as described in Chapter 3.

The first Pegasus was constructed in Ferranti's central London premises (Figure 2.9), thus (significantly for some) at a 200-mile distance from the higher-performance Ferranti Mercury design activity taking place concurrently at Ferranti's home ground in Manchester.

Between mid-1953 and early 1956, the Ferranti Pegasus engineering team in London grew from about ten to 30 people. Besides the four or five staff who had transferred from Borehamwood, the Pegasus engineering team now included Brian Maudsley, Ian Merry, Harry Metcalfe and John Fairclough. On NRDC's side, Christopher Strachey was joined at various times by others, such as Colin Merton and Donald Gillies, to work on low-level software and specimen applications alongside George Felton and others from Ferranti.

In October 1955 the first Pegasus ran its first program, using nickel delay line storage because the magnetic drum store, though connected to the

Figure 2.9 The first Pegasus computer, installed in the Ferranti Computer Centre at 21 Portland Place, London. The main computer consists of three bays. In this photograph, the doors of the first and third bays have been opened to reveal the rows of packaged electronic circuits. The lowest section of the left-hand bay contains the drum memory. The input-output equipment, consisting of paper-tape readers, a tape punch and a printer, are situated to the left of the photograph. This first Pegasus computer ran a user service from April 1956 to the summer of 1969. (Photo courtesy of Ferranti archive and ICL.)

computer, was still in the final stages of engineering development. The drum was working and in use by programmers by mid-March 1956. Production of subsequent Pegasus machines was carried out in Ferranti's West Gorton factory in Manchester under the direction of Brian Pollard. Although there was some initial misunderstanding between London, Manchester and NRDC over project costs, which blighted initial sales prospects, the Pegasus project turned out to be a real success story for Ferranti Ltd and for John Crawley, the pivotal NRDC person who oversaw the contracts from the earliest days.

The first Pegasus was in full operation, running a service to external customers in Ferranti's Computer Centre, Portland Place, London, from April 1956 onwards. This first Pegasus machine continued in service until the summer of 1969. A listing of all 40 Pegasus computers built is given in Chapter 4. The establishment of Ferranti's London Computer Centre, and its beneficial effect upon sales prospects for Pegasus, is an interesting development to which we will return. However, we first need to describe the hardware and software of Pegasus.

3 Technical description of the Ferranti Pegasus

3.1 Overall design objectives

Quoting from the Ferranti in-house journal of the time, the philosophy behind the design of Pegasus was to produce a computer with the following characteristics:

(a) easy to use;

(b) extremely reliable;

(c) easy to produce in quantity;

(d) in the medium price range.

To place requirement (a) in context, 'ease of use' in 1953 meant 'ease of programming the computer in machine code'. These were the days before high-level languages and before operating systems, so programmers had virtually no 'pre-installed' software to shield them from the basic hardware. Users had to code up lists of instructions chosen from a repertoire of simple arithmetic and logical primitives. Since programmers were usually trained mathematicians working on the solution of problems in numerical analysis, the need to break a problem down into primitive arithmetic and logical steps did not in itself present much difficulty. It was the additional complications, such as having to specify parameters in an instruction which depended upon hardware timings and internal storage organisation, that caused programmers to describe some computers as harder to use than others. Thanks to Christopher Strachey's influence, Pegasus had no such complications. As explained below, Pegasus had what we would now recognise as a powerful, symmetrical, general-register instruction set with modest support for memory management.

To place requirement (b) in context, namely that Pegasus should be reliable, remember that occasional hardware malfunction was a fact of life for computers in 1953. Indeed, users were cautious about the correctness of computations and often built elaborate cross-checking into their programs. It was not unknown for large calculations to be repeated three times and results to be accepted only when any two runs agreed. It was common for an installation to lose a couple of hours or more in a 24-hour period while an unexpected fault was traced and rectified by the on-site maintenance engineers. On Pegasus, a high standard of circuit design helped to minimise the occurrence of faults. The next step was therefore to ensure that any faults were quickly identified and rectified. Pegasus employed robust circuit packages, automatic parity checking of data transfers and diagnostics using voltage margins, to minimise the time taken to identify and fix hardware faults. These technological aspects are explained in more detail in Section 3.3.

As a measure of the Pegasus reliability actually achieved, statistics were gathered over a period of weeks of the useful time expressed as a percentage of the scheduled operational time. For the eight weeks to 23 March 1957, the fourth production Pegasus computer returned a figure of just over 99 per cent reliability. Such evidence astounded users of other contemporary UK computers.

The above comments are sufficient to suggest that hardware issues were of more than casual interest to users of early computers. We return to the hardware of Pegasus in Section 3.3. First, we give a programmer's view of the instruction set and central registers. The following account is for a standard Pegasus 1 machine; minor differences for the Pegasus 2 variant are noted as they occur.

3.2 The instruction set and memory organisation

Pegasus is a serial computer with a fixed-length word of 39 bits, plus three extra bits invisible to software. When used as data, the 39-bit word represents a fixed-point two's complement binary number (representing either an integer or a fraction in the range: $-1 \leq x < +1$). When a word is used for program code, two 19-bit instructions plus a stop/go bit are packed into each word. If the stop/go bit is set to zero by a programmer, the computer will halt before executing the instructions in the word; if it is a '1', execution proceeds at full speed. Restarting after a halt is under the control of a switch on the Pegasus control desk.

For the main computational orders, a Pegasus instruction consists of four fields labelled N, X, F and M, as shown in Table 3.1. N can be interpreted as

Table 3.1 The Pegasus 19-bit instruction format for the main computational orders

N	X	F	M
address or constant	accumulator	op.code	modifier (index register)
7 bits	3 bits	6 bits	3 bits

19

Figure 3.1 The first Ferranti Pegasus was designed and assembled in London and installed at the Ferranti Computer Centre in Portland Place. This first Pegasus supported four activities: demonstrations to prospective customers, programmer training, software development, and a computing service for paying clients. The photograph shows program development in progress, with a Pegasus paper tape reader in the right foreground. (Photo courtesy of Ferranti archive and ICL.)

an address or as an immediate operand (literal, or constant). Operand addresses are optionally modified by the addition of the contents of a specified modifier register, M. The modifier register actually contains two fields: an index and a count. The index is 13 bits which, when representing an address in the main (drum) store, consist of a ten-bit block address M_b followed by a 3-bit position address M_p. Once a block of data is in the fast computing store, address-modification uses only the M_p bits.

The total addressable memory is divided into two physical sections:

(a) the fast-access computing store, implemented as nickel delay lines; addressing provision was made for up to 128 words (approximately 640 bytes) of computing store, though only 48 words plus the 7 accumulators plus 15 special locations (see below) were implemented.

(b) the slower-access main store, implemented as a magnetic drum; this has a physical capacity of 5120 words, divided as follows: 4096 words (approximately 20 kbytes) of read/write user-space; 512 words of write-protected space in which is kept the program input system known as Initial Orders, and another 512 words of write-protected space in which engineers' test programs are stored.

For addressing purposes, both the computing store and the main store are logically divided into eight-word blocks. It is made easy for a programmer to transfer blocks of information between main and fast stores. The arrangement for address-modification and the provision of a special increment, test and jump instruction assume that computation will normally progress on a block of data at a time. By these means, Pegasus provides the user with consistent support for a software-implemented unified memory system. An example is given later.

In parenthesis, the memory capacity of Pegasus looks absurdly small to modern eyes. However, in contemporary terms 4000 words of main store was regarded as 'ample'. The six blocks of fast computing store, plus seven accumulators, were also felt to be quite sufficient. A contemporary account states: 'Generally, three blocks will be used for [structured] data and results, one for counters and [local] variables, and two for programme [instructions]. Often this allocation is not kept to, and in simple programmes several blocks may well be left unused.'

Since the computing store and the central registers are implemented as a collection of single-word nickel delay lines, this section of Pegasus' memory is random-access (i.e. functionally similar to modern RAM). The central

Table 3.2 Address map for the Pegasus fast store. Computing store addresses 64 to 111 in the table are identified in the form Block.Position, running from 0.0 through to 5.7. The eight accumulators, denoted as X0–X7, can each be used either for computation or for address-modification and loop-counting. X0 is always zero. Accumulators X6 and X7 act as a double-length pair p,q during certain multiply, divide, and shift instructions. The full Pegasus instruction set is given in Table 3.3.

Decimal address	Program notation	Description
0 → 7	0 → 7	accumulators, $X0$–$X7$. ($X0$ is always zero)
8 → 14	–	(unassigned: always contain zero)
15	15	handswitches (20 bits)
16	16	input/output (5 bits, checked)
17	17	input/output (5 bits, unchecked)
18 → 31	–	(unassigned: always contain zero)
32	32	constant (-1.0)
33	33	constant (1/2)
34	34	constant (2^{-10})
35	35	constant (2^{-13})
36 → 63	–	(unassigned: always contain zero)
64 → 111	0.0 → 5.7	48 words for program/data, as 6 blocks of 8 words each
112 → 127	–	(unassigned: always contain zero)

processing unit's registers are memory-mapped – that is to say, they can be addressed directly in instructions. The full range of addresses within the computing store is usefully viewed, according to modern terminology, as the mappings shown in Table 3.2. Code and data may be swapped under program control between the faster computing store (nickel delay lines) and the slower main store (magnetic drum). The data paths within the central processing unit (CPU) are very similar to a modern general-register computer. Translating into modern terminology, all the possible paths taken by data – that is, operands – in Pegasus during computation are conceptually as shown in Figure 3.2.

The instruction set (or order code, as it was called in the mid-1950s) has 49 valid functions (operations). The complete list, plus explanation, is given in Table 3.3. To summarise, the instructions divide into four functional groups:

a) simple arithmetic and logical operations (op.codes 00–07, 10–17, 40–47):
   load/store (both positively and negatively);
   add, subtract, reverse-subtract;
   AND; exclusive OR.

b) Multiply, divide, shift, and normalise operations (op.codes 20–27, 50–57).

c) Control transfers (jumps) and counting (op.codes 60–67).

d) Reading/writing from/to drum; select I/O device; stop.

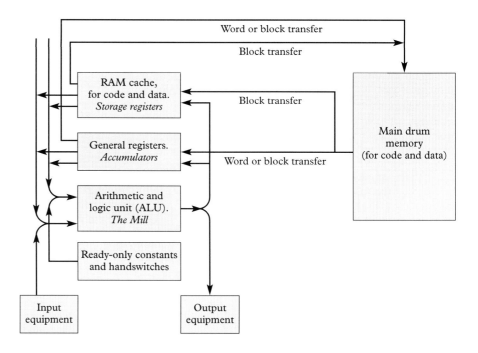

Figure 3.2 Conceptual paths for operands in Pegasus, expressed in modern terminology. (Pegasus terminology in italics.)

Group (a) was remarkable in 1954 for its symmetry, allowing both stored and literal (immediate) operands to be exchanged between all locations/registers in the computing store's address space. The accumulator registers can be used for computation, address-modification (indexing), and for loop-control counting. The general forms of an add instruction are: $N + X \rightarrow X$ or $N + X \rightarrow N$. Historically, this symmetry and flexibility made the Pegasus architecture an important landmark in computer design. We can now see that Christopher Strachey influenced the instruction set of many subsequent machines.

Character-by-character input/output is also achieved via group (a) instructions. The standard input device for Pegasus is a 200 character-per-second (char./sec.), five-track, paper-tape reader. The standard output device is a 33 char./sec. paper-tape punch, the tape from which is usually led across directly to a teleprinter which prints at 7 char./sec. By means of the 'set I/O device mode' instruction, other external serial character devices could be selected. Magnetic tape drives or punched-card equipment was controlled by additional hardware which contained buffer storage. During its production

Table 3.3 Instruction set (order code) for Pegasus

00	x' = n (*n is contents of an addr*)		40	x' = c (c is an 8-bit signed number (*literal*)).
01	x' = x + n		41	x' = x + c
02	x' = – n		42	x' = – c
03	x' = x – n		43	x' = x – c
04	x' = n – x		44	x' = c – x
05	x' = x & n		45	x' = x & c
06	x' = x *XOR* n		46	x' = x *XOR* c
07			47	
10	n' = x		50	x' = 2^Nx arithmetic shift
11	n' = n + x		51	x' = 2^{-N}x rounded shift
12	n' = – x		52	Shift x up N places (logical shift)
13	n' = n – x		53	Shift x down N places (logical shift)
14	n' = x – n		54	(pq)' = 2^N(pq)
15	n' = n & x		55	(pq)' = 2^{-N} (pq) unrounded
16	n' = n *XOR* x		56	(pq)' = 2^μ (pq); x' = x – $2^{-38}\mu$; normalise
17			57	
20	Multiply: (pq)' = n.x		60	Jump if x = 0
21	Multiply and round–off in X6: p' = $(n.x)_r$		61	Jump if x ≠ 0
22	Multiply and add: (pq)' = n.x + (pq)		62	Jump if x ≥ 0
23	Justify (nq)		63	Jump if x < 0
24	Divide, unrounded: q' = (xq)/n. p' = remainder		64	Jump if overflow clear
25	Divide, rounded: q' = $[(xq)/n]_r$. p' = remainder		65	Jump if overflow set, and clear
26	Divide, rounded, q' = $[x/n]_r$		66	Unit-modify: increment modifier & jump if x_p ≠ 0.
27			67	Unit-count: decrement counter & jump if ≠ 0.
30			70	Single-word read from main (drum) store to X1.
31			71	Single-word write to main (drum) store from X1.
32			72	Block read from main (drum) store
33			73	Block write to main (drum) store
34			74	Select input/output device (external switching).
35			75	
36			76	
37			77	Stop

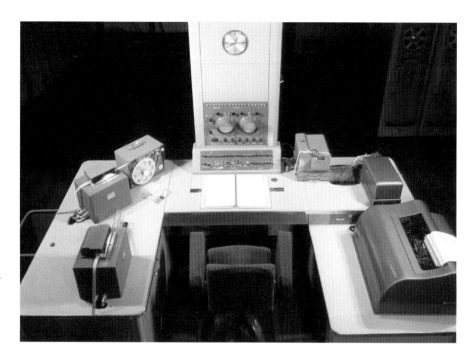

Figure 3.3 A bird's-eye view of the Pegasus operating console. On the table-top to the left are two paper-tape readers and a tape spooler. To the right are a paper-tape punch and a printer sub-system. Basically, paper tape containing code and data is fed in on the left-hand side and results appear on the right. In front, the control panel contains two circular display-screens and many switches, for use in manually debugging a program and for engineers' fault-finding procedures. For example, a programmer may cause Pegasus to execute instructions singly under manual control, whilst the contents of selected memory locations are displayed on the screens. (Photo courtesy of Ferranti archive and ICL.)

life (1956–62) two kinds of (mutually incompatible) punched-card equipment were interfaced to particular Pegasus computers, as explained in Chapter 4.

By means of four instructions in group (d), single-word or block read/write transfers are initiated between the computing store and the drum. Blocks of eight words are the usual form of transfer. The programmer normally regards the computing store as containing six eight-word blocks and the drum as containing 512 eight-word blocks of usable space. Since there were no hardware aids to memory partitioning such as datum/limit registers, Pegasus programmers have to organise their own scheme of overlays. However, the counter/modifier facilities help in achieving position-independent relocation.

Besides the stop/go bit mentioned previously, Pegasus provides other hardware-assisted debugging aids for the programmer. These aids are available via switches and displays on the machine's front console (control desk; see Figure 3.3). The debugging facilities include single-stepping through a program one instruction at a time, and the ability to examine the contents of the eight accumulators and each storage location in the fast memory. An instruction is displayed on the console in an easy-to-understand form, with the op.code and address fields presented as octal digits.

3.3 Hardware details

3.3.1 Overall construction

A Pegasus computer is made up of cabinets of electronics, conveniently divided into sections known as bays, which are 71 cm wide and 76 cm long, and a control desk which includes the paper-tape input/output equipment. The design is modular. The original Pegasus 1 was a three-bay computer, shown in Figure 2.9 (page 17), but the Pegasus on display in the Science Museum in London is a four-bay computer with refrigeration ducts (such as the one seen in Figure 3.4). Both systems also have a two-bay power supply unit, fed with regulated electricity by a mains-driven motor-alternator set.

Pegasus uses a total of 15 kW of electrical power, of which the actual computing circuits consume 7 kW. Within the central computer, most of the power is used by the thermionic valve ('tube') heaters. By control of the alternator excitation, the power to the valve heaters is brought up slowly for two minutes upon first switching Pegasus on, thereby increasing reliability by not imposing excessive thermal shocks to the valves. The heat dissipated

Figure 3.4 A larger, more powerful, four-bay Pegasus 2 computer. Although the provision of magnetic tape decks (seen in the background to the left) and multiple printers (shown to the right) enhanced the appeal of Pegasus to the commercial data processing market, the business community was more interested in systems based on punched-card input rather than paper-tape input. Accordingly, an extra unit called a converter could be added to a Pegasus 2 installation. The converter coupled the Pegasus magnetic tape system to punched-card readers and punches, and to high-speed line-printers. (Photo courtesy of Ferranti archive and ICL.)

within a basic Pegasus was normally removed by forced-air cooling driven by fans in the base. The forced-air system was designed to be easily replaced by a refrigeration system, in the case of large installations or poorly ventilated sites.

Ease of fault detection, location and repair was a design objective for Pegasus. Parity checking is performed on all transfers to/from the drum and the nickel delay line stores; this means that single-bit errors are detected at run-time, should they occur. All Pegasus installations also had some scheduled maintenance time during each 24-hour period. During maintenance, engineers' test programs could be run and the high-tension (HT) voltage supplies to sub-sections of the machine could be selectively altered manually by (say) + or –10 per cent of nominal. This so-called marginal testing shows up incipient faults, such as those due to deteriorating thermionic valves (tubes), before they manifest themselves under normal HT voltage conditions.

It was a characteristic of all Pegasus computers that the outer casings of the cabinets had tastefully curved edges and corners and a very good quality of finish. The company responsible for the bodywork was H J Mulliner, coachbuilders, of Park Royal, London – the same company that carried out skilled work on Rolls-Royce and Bentley cars. The Pegasus blue-grey gloss finish was obtained with about ten coats of 'Valentine's Special Lavender No. 2' paint, rubbed down lovingly between each coat. The doors close with that luxurious Rolls-Royce clunk.

3.3.2 The Pegasus memory systems

The fast (computing) store uses nickel delay line technology. All acoustic delay line storage systems depend upon the fact that the velocity of ultrasonic pulses in material such as mercury or nickel is very much slower than the velocity of electrical pulses in copper wire. If we arrange to convert digital information (as electrical signals) into sound waves (i.e. shock waves), then the digital information (now in ultrasonic form) will take a relatively long time to travel through the mercury or nickel. During the period while the information is thus delayed, or 'stored', we could be getting on with other computational activity.

Each Pegasus nickel delay line works as follows. A transmitting transducer, T, converts an incoming signal into a sonic pulse, which travels along a nickel wire. A receiving transducer, R, detects the transmitted sound pulse and transforms it back into electrical form. An electronic circuit couples the receiver back to the transmitter to give a recirculating memory. The delay between T and R depends upon the length of the nickel path and the speed

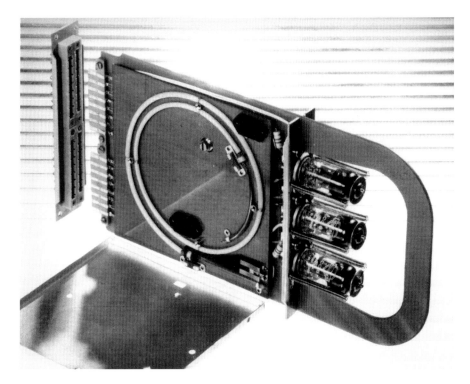

Figure 3.5 A Pegasus one-word (42-digit) nickel delay-line memory, with cover removed. The reverse side of this circuit package is shown in Figure 3.7. The 60 cm of nickel wire, in a plastic sleeve, has been formed into a 12 cm diameter coil and the whole package is about the size of a paperback book. Many of these delay lines formed Pegasus' fast (random access) computing store. The unit pictured used longitudinal stress waves in the nickel wire; later Pegasus systems used torsional waves. (Photo courtesy of the Museum of Science and Industry in Manchester.)

of sound in nickel. If $n \times t$ is the delay, then n digits each separated by time t can be stored. Most Pegasus nickel delay lines store 42 bits (one word plus a parity bit plus two padding digits) with a digit time of three microseconds. A piece of nickel wire about 60 cm long is sufficient to store 42 digits, each separated by three microseconds (see Figure 3.5).

The velocity of longitudinal sound (stress) waves in materials such as nickel and mercury is temperature-dependent. In the case of nickel, the thermal coefficient is relatively small and there is no need for special temperature control. In the case of mercury, a close control has to be kept of the temperature of a mercury delay line storage system.

The original Pegasus nickel delay lines used longitudinal stress waves. These tended to suffer from signal dispersion problems in long lines, although the Borehamwood Nicholas had used 128-word longitudinal delay lines with reasonable results. John Bennett, working in Ferranti's London laboratories, suggested that torsional waves would overcome the dispersion problems.

Gordon Scarrott, from 1953 the chief research engineer in Ferranti's Manchester Computer Department, confirmed this. He devised a method of welding short pieces of nickel tape tangentially to long steel wires so that longitudinal waves, introduced and detected magnetostrictively in the nickel, would generate torsional waves in the steel wire. The arrangement worked well and opened up the possibility of having reliable delay lines that would hold many words. The torsional arrangement was used in later Pegasus machines, and in the Ferranti Perseus and Sirius computers.

The Pegasus main store is based on a magnetically-coated drum (Figure 3.6), on whose surface digital information can be recorded. This is similar in principle to a modern PC's hard disk, except that the Pegasus drum has a fixed read/write head for each information track – thereby reducing the access time. A Pegasus drum contains 5120 words (each 42 digits), of which 1024 are locked out (privileged access) since these contain the Initial Orders, Assembly subroutines and engineers' test programs. Ian Merry was responsible for the design of the drum.

For addressing purposes, the drum is divided into 40 logical tracks, each 128 words (i.e. 16 eight-word blocks). Actually, odd and even digits are written to a pair of physical tracks on the drum's surface, with a head per physical track. There is a logical address track which gives the drum's current

Figure 3.6 A Pegasus drum store, measuring approximately 25 cm in diameter and 16 cm in length. The revolution time of the drum (3720 r.p.m.) is controlled electronically, with reference to a crystal oscillator. The drum has a clock track, which generates the clocking pulses for the Pegasus central processor. Arranging for the drum to dictate the processor's timing made it easier to achieve synchronisation and reliable transfers of information. In contrast, the (multiple) drums on the Ferranti Mark I Star and Mercury computers were synchronised to the processor's clock pulses. (Photo courtesy of the Museum of Science and Industry in Manchester.).

position as a 128-word address. It is arranged that logically-adjacent block-addresses are stored in physical positions separated by two blocks on the drum's surface. This interleaving enables successively numbered blocks to be read or written back sequentially with a small amount of intervening computation. For much of the time, a programmer could therefore read or write successively-numbered blocks at optimum speed – another example of how Pegasus users could achieve high performance without having to worry about underlying hardware details.

Early Pegasus drums each held 5120 words. A larger 9216-word drum was introduced at a later stage and became standard on Pegasus 2 machines. Also, part of the drum's contents was later placed in an 'Intermediate Access Store' consisting of long (336-bit, i.e. eight-word) torsional nickel delay lines.

3.3.3 *The central processing unit (CPU) and package technology*

The main Pegasus logic circuits use thermionic valves and germanium diodes operating at a clock frequency of 333 kHz. Although several computers in the mid-1950s employed replaceable sub-assemblies, the Pegasus circuits are interesting because they are mounted on relatively small sub-units, or 'packages' (see Figure 3.7), which are handy for quick replacement in the event of repairs being necessary.

There are 444 plug-in packages in total, consisting of 20 standard types, in a three-bay Pegasus 1 computer. Of these 444 packages, 314 contain the CPU's logic circuits, of which there are only five standard types. The remaining 130 packages contain the nickel delay lines, drum store amplifiers, input/output interface circuits, clock/reset waveform circuits, etc. The four-bay Pegasus on display in the Science Museum in London contains 604 packages, but some of these are for input/output devices no longer connected.

In designing the circuits for the Ferranti Pegasus, Charles Owen took a fresh look at the packaging concept. He studied the variability in the nominal characteristics of standard electronic components and devised mathematical techniques to determine the effects of component deviations. In this way, the design of reliable circuits for Pegasus was made easier. The logical structure of Pegasus was then carefully analysed to work out how best to divide it into functional types of package. The choice of logic building blocks was then generalised. The intention of Bill Elliott's team was that, once established, the repertoire of Pegasus packages would be used in a variety of computers and their control units for ancillary equipment such as magnetic tapes.

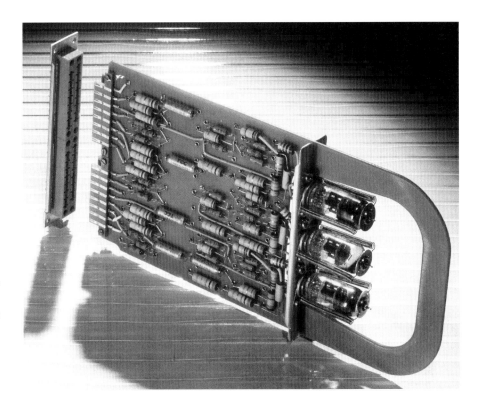

Figure 3.7 A Pegasus circuit package, with three type-12AT7 thermionic triode valves positioned near the handle. The other electronic components on the main part of the package are semiconductor (germanium) diodes and resistors. Diode–resistor circuits are used to implement simple logical functions on binary digits. All of the central processor's arithmetical and control operations are implemented by combinations of only five basic types of circuit package. This considerably eased the task of manufacturing Pegasus computers in quantity, and of repairing and replacing any faulty packages in the field. Pegasus installations achieved impressive reliability figures compared with other computers of the 1950s. (Photo courtesy of the Museum of Science and Industry in Manchester.)

This meant that new input/output controllers for Pegasus could be implemented speedily, without the need for circuit prototyping.

The validity of the plug-in package concept was questioned in some quarters in the mid-1950s, because of its reliance on the correct electro-mechanical operation of connectors. Brian Maudsley devised a distinctive system of contacts plated with a noble metal, in which the socket-element scraped a minute layer from the plug-element each time they were mated. This avoided problems due to oxidisation of the contact surfaces.

Another mid-1950s criticism of the package philosophy was that it would lead to hardware redundancy. In practice, the redundancy on Pegasus was estimated to amount to about 10 per cent extra packages. A final criticism was that the separate packages would introduce variations in pulse amplitudes and delays that would call for a great deal of adjustment. By conservative choice of pulse frequency, the need for local adjustments was avoided.

In conclusion, Bill Elliott's team at Ferranti had produced a well-engineered machine. Charles Owen's skill as a computer engineer was subsequently recognised at IBM, where he became an IBM Fellow.

3.3.4 Instruction timing

Pegasus has a 333 kHz clock, so that the digit-period is three microseconds. To the 39-bit programmer's word are added three extra hardware bits, invisible to software, namely: a parity digit and two gap digits. Therefore, a Pegasus word-time is $42 \times 3 = 126$ microseconds. Each basic arithmetic operation took two word-times; instruction-fetch took one word-time. Since two instructions were packed in each word, a pair of additions (e.g. op.code 11) took the following times:

Fetch a pair of add instructions	126 microseconds.
Execute first addition	252 microseconds.
Execute second addition	252 microseconds.

Therefore, the time for a single add is 630/2 microseconds. The time for an addition is usually quoted in the Pegasus literature as 0.3 milliseconds. Multiplication is 2.0 milliseconds; division is 5.4 milliseconds. Drum transfers took 9 milliseconds on average. Typical times for small sections of program, including software-implemented floating-point operations, are given in Section 3.5. For floating-point representation, Pegasus normally uses a 30-bit mantissa and a nine-bit exponent (base 2).

The very modest Pegasus clock-rate of 333 kHz was a happy legacy from a pre-1950, pre-401, Borehamwood design for a CRT-based memory system (see Section 2.2). The rate of 333 kHz allowed Pegasus to use cheaper thermionic valves than, for example, the NPL Pilot ACE computer. First operational in May 1950, the Pilot ACE had a clock-rate of 1 MHz and was generally considered to be the fastest of the early British computers. However, the Pilot ACE's addition time could vary between 64 micro-seconds and 1.024 milliseconds, depending upon the position of instruction and operands. One contemporary benchmarking exercise rated the Ferranti Mark I at about the same raw power as the NPL Pilot ACE, even though the latter had a clock-rate ten times as fast. The favourable performance of the Ferranti Mark I was attributed to its random access memory and its fast multiplier. Other tests indicate that the Pilot ACE was faster than the Mark I, but scarcely by as much as a factor of ten. Then, as now, clock-rate is unsatisfactory as a single indicator of useful computer performance. We return to the subject of comparative performance in Chapter 5.

3.4 Specimen programs for Pegasus

The Pegasus instruction set lent itself to a straightforward two-digit representation of op.codes, which was easy to remember. There was thus less need for a symbolic assembler than on many other early computers. Each Pegasus instruction is typed on one line in the form:

N X F M (but M may be omitted if zero, i.e. if no address-modification).

Thus, for example:

4.1 2 01 3   adds the content of block 4 line 1 modified by accumulator 3 to accumulator 2. Instructions, as written by a programmer, are entirely numeric but letters are used to introduce directives, which cause Initial Orders (see below) to carry out various operations on input or output. Thus the directive D causes the date to be printed followed by a serial number for the run; R indicates a subroutine call (or 'cue'). There was a comprehensive subroutine library for Pegasus – see later. An Assembly system enabled the user to select library subroutines on input, from a separate library paper tape, as now described.

Booting up an empty machine was a simple process because the so-called Initial Orders were stored permanently on the drum. A user invoked these Initial Orders by operating the 'Start' and 'Run' switches on the computer's control console. The five-track paper tapes on which user programs are punched are read by Initial Orders. Included in Initial Orders is the Assembly system, which recognises calls for subroutines from the letter R preceding them. At the end of program input, Assembly collects specified standard subroutines from the library tape placed in the second paper-tape reader, and inserts appropriate cues so that the subroutines can be entered from the program when required. When the program has been assembled, an Enter directive such as E 2.0 will transfer control to the program at the specified address. Subsequent operation, including data input, is controlled by the user program by calling subroutines when required. Once a program has been assembled as described above, it can be punched out in a compact binary form on a single paper tape for fast input on subsequent runs.

All this is best illustrated by a simple example program (see Table 3.4) which calculates and prints a table of powers of the numbers 1 to 20. The machine-code program, i.e. the left-hand column of Table 3.4, would have been prepared off-line by typing the characters into a teleprinter, which produces five-track paper tape. Figure 3.8 shows a photograph of a tape editing set; this is an example of what became known later as 'data preparation

Figure 3.8 An off-line, five-track, paper-tape editing set used by Pegasus programmers. The device on the left produces both printed paper and punched paper tape. When an operator types instructions and/or data on the keyboard, both a printed listing and a length of tape are produced. The punched tape is then normally fed into Pegasus (see Figure 3.3). Any piece of punched tape can also be interpreted by placing it in the device on the right of the desk, which senses the patterns of holes and sends characters electrically to the device on the left for printing and, if required, re-punching. Using stop/start/skip switches, erroneous tapes can be edited. (Photo courtesy of Ferranti archive and ICL.)

equipment'. The punched paper tape containing the program of Table 3.4 would then be fed manually into a 200 character-per-second paper-tape reader which was connected to Pegasus. During computation, the program produces output in the form of punched paper tape which, when fed manually into a teleprinter, produces the printed results shown in Table 3.5.

The simple program of Table 3.4 does not use address modification. In Table 3.6 we give a program fragment that illustrates the ingenious Pegasus facilities for address modification, drum transfers and special jump instructions. The sequence adds up 213 numbers, which are initially stored in 213 consecutive locations in the main (drum) memory, beginning at address 300.5. Table 3.6 assumes that address 0.0 (meaning line 0 of block 0) in the fast computing store has previously been loaded with (300.5, 213) – i.e. a word with 300.5 in the modifier position and 213 in the counter position. We assume that block 4.0 in the fast computing store is the (overlaid) destination for successive blocks of data being read from the drum. We also assume that the program is entered at position 0.1, and that the answer to the summation is required in line 0 of block 5 of the fast store at the conclusion.

Table 3.4 A simple Pegasus program to calculate and print a table of powers. The machine-code program, i.e. the left-most columns of numbers and letters, would have been prepared offline by these characters being typed into the teleprinter device shown in Figure 3.8. The teleprinter produces punched paper tape and is part of what was known as a tape editing set, or data preparation equipment. The resulting length of five-track paper tape was then fed into a Pegasus paper-tape reading device shown in Figure 3.3.

Program			Annotations for Pegasus program sheet
D			Print Date when program run
N			Print the following program Name

SIMPLE LIST OF POWERS

A1			Call Assembly Routine for Library Subroutines
R0	3	-08	Place cue 8 to subroutine R4 (Number Print) in B2.3
4	-	01-	(3 locations beyond default start address B2.0)
20	3	40	Set count for 20 numbers in $X3$
1	5	40	Set first number $n = 1$ in $X5$
6	2	40	Set 6 in $X2$ to print 6 digits of number
5	7	00	Copy current number n from $X5$ to $X7$
4	4	40	Set count of 4 in $X4$ for powers up to 4
0.4	1	02	Set link for R4, negative to print on new line
+0			Space for Cue 08 for R4, to print integer from $X7$
2	0	72	Link for return from R4, Drum Block 2 to U0
0.5	0	60	Jump to U0.5 (U = Working Store Address)
5	7	20	Multiply by n to form next power
0.4	1	00	Set link for R4, positive to print on same line
0.3	4	67	Count powers, jump to 0.3 to print next power
1	5	41	Increase n in $X5$ by 1
0.1	3	67	Count numbers n, jump to 0.1 for next n
0	0	77	Stop at end of program
A2			Read subroutine library, to obtain R4
A3			Add subroutine cue to program
N			Print the following title sequence

TABLE OF POWERS OF n

n	n^2	n^3	n^4

J2.0	Call Program from Block 2 and enter at U0.0

A program called PEGEM which simulates the operation of Pegasus has been developed, together with comprehensive documentation and a tutorial for writing and running a simple Pegasus program. The program runs on a personal computer under MSDOS. The main feature of the program is that the user is presented with a 'virtual Pegasus', that is a graphical representation of the control panels, monitor displays and peripherals of the original machine. The user can then move an image of a hand with outstretched finger to operate the switches and handle the paper tapes. The Pegasus program library, test programs and a set of demonstration programs are provided, and many users have commented that they really do

Table 3.5 *Powers of* n *produced by the program of Table 3.4*

n	n²	n³	n⁴
1	1	1	1
2	4	8	16
3	9	27	81
4	16	64	256
5	25	125	625
6	36	216	1296
7	49	343	2401
8	64	512	4096
9	81	729	6561
10	100	1000	10000
11	121	1331	14641
12	144	1728	20736
13	169	2197	28561
14	196	2744	38416
15	225	3375	50625
16	256	4096	65536
17	289	4913	83521
18	324	5832	104976
19	361	6859	130321
20	400	8000	160000

Table 3.7 *A Pegasus Autocode program to calculate the root mean square (RMS) of the variables v1, v2, ... v100. F1 in the last line denotes a call to a built-in square root function.*

```
      n1 = 1
      v101 = 0
2)    v102 = vn1 × vn1
      v101 = v101 + v102
      n1 = n1 + 1
      →2, 100 ≥ n1
      v101 = v101/100
      v101 = SQRTv101
```

get the 'look and feel' of operating a real Pegasus. The simulator runs at approximately real speed on a fast '386 PC and upwards. (The simulator was developed by the Computer Conservation Cociety [CCS], and is available for downloading from the CCS ftp archive at: ftp.cs.man.ac.uk/pub/CCS-Archive/simulators/Pegasus or via the CCS web site at www.cs.man.ac.uk/CCS.)

3.5 *The Pegasus program library and Autocode system*

A feature of the customer support provided by Ferranti Ltd was the existence of a large library of subroutines – normally resident on paper tape or magnetic tape. Library tapes and documentation were updated as new facilities were added. By 1962 the library contained approximately 200 subroutines, plus a Matrix Interpretive Scheme and an Autocode.

The Matrix Interpretive Scheme, developed by George Felton (Figure 3.9) and others from about 1954, allowed large floating-point structures to be added, subtracted, copied, multiplied, divided, transposed and normalised with ease. Matrices are stored by columns in consecutive addresses (one word per element) in the main drum store. The convention adopted was that 1023 is added to a matrix address to obtain the corresponding drum address. A typical matrix instruction is:

$$(304, 10 \times 12) \times (1195, 12 \times 16) \rightarrow 5$$

When obeyed, this causes the matrix in address 304 with ten rows and 12 columns to be post-multiplied by the matrix in address 1195 with 12 rows and 16 columns; the resulting 10×16 matrix is placed in address five. This was all done in floating point and took about 42.4 seconds, according to the manual. Double-length and complex versions of floating-point arithmetic interpretive schemes also existed in the Pegasus program library.

Pegasus Autocode was developed by Brian Clarke and George Felton in 1956–57, based on Tony Brooker's Mark I Autocode which was available for the Ferranti Mark I computer at Manchester University from mid-1954. (For reference, the first FORTRAN user manual, entitled *The FORTRAN automatic coding system for the IBM 704 EDPM*, was dated October 1956). The Autocode was a primitive high-level language, in which variables were either floating-point (denoted as $v0$, $v1$, $v2$, ...) or integer ($n0$, $n1$, $n2$, ...). Intrinsic functions were denoted by capital letters, e.g. SQRT signified 'square root'. An Autocode sequence to calculate the root mean square (RMS) of the variables $v1$, $v2$, ... $v100$ could be written as shown in Table 3.7.

Table 3.6 *Program fragment showing drum transfers and address modification. The purpose is to sum the 213 numbers which are stored at addresses 300.5 onwards on the drum. The program assumes address 0.0 has previously been loaded with a word containing a modifier of 300.5 and a count of 213, and that address 0.1 is the entry point. Block 4 in the computing store is used for working space and the answer is placed in address 5.0.*

Addr.	Instruction	Comment
0.1	0 3 00	Clear $X3$ to receive the sum.
	0.0 2 00	Set $X2$ with a modifier of 300.5 and a count of 213.
0.2	0 4 72 2	Read first block from the drum.
	4.0 3 01 2	Start of loop: add one number into $X3$.
0.3	0.4 2 66	Incr. modifier and jump to 0.4 if position-part $\neq$ 0.
	0 4 72 2	Read next block from drum when needed.
0.4	0.2 + 2 67	Decr. counter & jump to 2nd order in word 0.2 if $\neq$ 0.
	5.0 3 10	Place the sum in first line of block 5 of fast store.

Figure 3.9 George Felton (born 1921). After wartime RAF radar work, Felton became a physics post-graduate at Cambridge University. There he attended the influential computing seminars organised by Professor Maurice Wilkes. After joining Borehamwood in 1951, Felton was responsible for the Nicholas programming system. Nicholas software was an extended form of the Cambridge EDSAC Initial Orders and subroutine library. From mid-1954 Felton led the Ferranti team developing innovative and comprehensive software for Pegasus and, later, Orion, a pioneering multi-tasking system. He continued his key role when Ferranti's computer interests were taken over by ICT (later ICL); the ICL 1900 series George operating systems are said to have been named after him. (Photo courtesy of George Felton.)

The Pegasus Autocode system was used for rapid programming of applications in which speed of operation was not critical.

Returning to the machine-code subroutines in the Pegasus library, some idea of the code size and speed of operation (in milliseconds) may be gained from descriptions of three standard subroutines:

R200 fixed-point square root: 1 block of code; time = 40 msec.

R211 floating-point cube root: 3 blocks of code; time = 103–149 msec.

R220 fixed-point exponential: 2 blocks of code; time = 29 msec.

A block of code is eight words, or 16 instructions, or approximately 40 bytes. Bearing in mind that Pegasus (in common with practically all computers of 1956) had no floating-point hardware, the compact code size is a reflection of the efficiency of the Pegasus instruction set. A software floating-point addition took 18 milliseconds.

4 Pegasus in action

4.1 Ferranti's organisation and marketing strategies

The Ferranti company was founded in 1882 by the inventor Sebastian de Ferranti (1864–1930) to manufacture electrical equipment of all types. By 1948 the company had built up a significant reputation in defence avionics and had started work on the successful Bloodhound guided weapon. On the electricity supply side, Ferranti was the major UK supplier of house-service meters and had secured about 25 per cent of the UK market for high-voltage power transformers. A Ferranti Computer Group was first set up in 1949 in the company's Instrument Division at Moston, Manchester, to manufacture the Ferranti Mark I computer for the University of Manchester under a special government contract. In 1951 the Computer Group began to make and sell computers on the open market – a process which continued until September 1963 when Ferranti Ltd sold its main computer business to International Computers and Tabulators (ICT). From February 1951 until the end of 1964 (when sales commitments came to an end) Ferranti Ltd built 102 computers of seven main types, namely: Mark I/Mark I Star, Pegasus 1/Pegasus 2, Mercury, Perseus, Orion 1/Orion 2, Sirius and Atlas. The smaller Ferranti Argus range of industrial control computers, and various special-purpose military machines, are not included in this list. Of the 102 larger computers manufactured by Ferranti, 22 were exported – but none reached the USA or Japan.

In June 1951 Bernard Swann joined Ferranti Ltd to team up with Vivian (later Lord) Bowden in marketing and selling Ferranti computers. It was Bernard Swann who directed the marketing strategy for the Ferranti Pegasus. The following comments on this strategy are based largely on Swann's 100-page *History of the Ferranti Computer Department*, written in 1975 and, out of loyalty to senior management, still unpublished.

Swann realised that Ferranti's hopes for increasing the company's computer sales in the mid-1950s depended upon:

a) an ability to branch out from their early UK successes within the scientific/research market, in order to tap the commercial/data processing market;

b) an ability to give live demonstrations of Ferranti machines running applications software relevant to each prospective customer.

Figure 4.1 The Pegasus production line at Ferranti's West Gorton factory in the autumn of 1956. This factory, in a district of east Manchester, was bought by Ferranti Ltd from a firm of textile machinery manufacturers. It was converted to become the new home for the Ferranti Computer Department, formerly at Moston near Manchester. The West Gorton factory contained what was, in 1956, the largest production line for computers in Europe. The photograph shows seven Pegasus computers and (in the background) three Mercury computers under construction. In 1968, West Gorton became the home of ICL's high-performance mainframe computer design and manufacture. (Photo courtesy of the Museum of Science and Industry in Manchester.)

Objective (a) requires a little more explanation. In 1955, no more than half a dozen commercial organisations in the UK had taken tentative steps towards applying electronic digital computers to office data processing. Most offices still relied entirely on manual processes assisted, in the larger organisations, by electro-mechanical equipment for sorting and tabulating data held on punched cards. Manufacturers of electro-mechanical punched-card equipment were well-entrenched in the commercial and business sector, so it was felt that the best way for Ferranti to achieve objective (a) was to enter into a liaison with one of the two main British punched-card companies. Ferranti chose Powers-Samas Accounting Machines Ltd ('Powers') rather than its rival, the British Tabulating Machine Company (BTM) who had obtained the UK marketing rights for punched-card machines developed in the USA by Herman Hollerith and IBM. The punched-card technologies used by Powers and by BTM were mutually incompatible, e.g. they used different-shaped holes in the cards and different coding of data. The arrangement between Ferranti and Powers lasted from October 1954 to July 1958. In July 1958 Powers-Samas and BTM decided to merge and become

Figure 4.2 The Ferranti Computer Centre at 21 Portland Place, London. This elegant house was built in 1777. The first famous person to live at number 21 was General Sir Henry Clinton, who was born in America in 1738. In 1778 Clinton was commander-in-chief of the British forces in America and was blamed by some for Britain's defeat in the War of Independence. The first Pegasus computer was assembled on the first floor of number 21 in 1955. (Photo courtesy of the Museum of Science and Industry in Manchester.)

a new company called International Computers and Tabulators (ICT). Due to fundamental differences in 'computing culture', marketing practice and delays in availability of suitable input/output equipment, the link between Ferranti and Powers-Samas was in the end not felt to have been very helpful to Ferranti's marketing efforts. As far as Pegasus was concerned, the tangible sign of the Ferranti–Powers arrangement was the Pluto variant: an advanced-feature Pegasus 1 to which a Powers card reader and punch were attached. Meanwhile, in response to a specific customer's requirement, a Pegasus 1 computer at the ICI Dyestuffs Division was modified by Ferranti to accept BTM punched-card equipment and US-supplied magnetic tape decks. Other Ferranti hardware developments in the commercial data processing field are discussed in Chapter 5.

Objective (b) – an ability to demonstrate to prospective customers – was greatly enhanced by a decision towards the end of 1952 to open a Ferranti Computer Centre in London. The view, amply justified by subsequent events, was that few of the important decision-makers in the south of England were prepared to undertake a round-trip of perhaps 400 miles to see a machine at Manchester. These were the days when all major UK public-sector and private-sector enterprises had their headquarters in London. Ferranti therefore decided to rent and repair a bomb-damaged, elegant, four-storey London house to the north of Oxford Street: number 21 Portland Place (Figure 4.2). Ferranti moved into Portland Place in 1954 – originally with the intention of installing a Mark I Star computer there. However, it soon became clear that a Pegasus would be more appropriate from a marketing viewpoint.

During 1955 the 'elegant house' (it had been built by the Adams Brothers in 1777) was prepared for the installation of the first Pegasus computer. The notion of a computer centre was new to the UK; its full potential evolved gradually. The original Ferranti plans for Portland Place called for a staff of ten programmers, five engineers and ten other staff. Five years later, upwards of 60 staff were accommodated and there were 50 to 80 visitors every week. The tasks of this London Computer Centre for Pegasus were fourfold: to interest potential purchasers by demonstrating how their kind of applications programs could be easily and reliably run on Pegasus; to hold regular two-week programming courses (Figure 4.4); to act as a focal point for the development, documentation and dissemination of a library of useful Pegasus software; and to run a computing service for paying customers. In all of these activities, Portland Place set new standards for what might now be called 'user support'. Besides spear-heading Pegasus marketing, Portland

Figure 4.3 Some members of the Pegasus engineering design team at Portland Place in 1955. From left to right: Charles Owen, Peter Dorey (in Bill Elliott's team but working on a defence contract rather than on Pegasus), Hugh Devonald, Harry Metcalfe, Stan Willis, (two people as yet unidentified), Ivan Idelson, (one unidentified person), Brian Nolan. This photograph was taken at about the time of a demonstration of Pegasus to the Press in October 1955. No members of the Pegasus software team are shown in this particular photograph.

Place also generated income: by 1962, there were over 150 paying customers using the Ferranti Computing Service.

A few words should be said about the cost of Pegasus, since this topic was the cause of much heated debate at the time. In about 1954, based on estimates of the manufacturing costs of Pegasus, the Ferranti staff believed that a selling price of about £32,000 would be sensible. This figure of £32,000 lay somewhere between the quoted price of an Elliott 401 and an English Electric Deuce, and was about one-third the price of a Ferranti Mark I Star. NRDC originally hoped that the Pegasus selling price would come out below £30,000, but agreed to the slightly higher figure. In the autumn of 1954 NRDC had undertaken to support Ferranti in the manufacture of an initial batch of ten Pegasus machines, but required in return a proportion of the selling price. (NRDC's terms of reference, from the government, required NRDC to make a modest operating profit, which was to be ploughed back into further projects.) Seemingly, NRDC was satisfied at the time with the calculation of Pegasus manufacturing costs and mark-up for overheads. Unfortunately, as manufacture at Manchester progressed, the estimated mark-up was judged by the Manchester division to be inadequate. As sales of the first few Pegasus were being confirmed (in 1955/6), the price was

Figure 4.4 A programming course in progress at the Ferranti Computer Centre in Portland Place. George Felton is seen lecturing on the Pegasus square root subroutine, part of a library of approximately 200 useful subroutines provided to make life easy for the applications programmer. The first Pegasus programming course was held from 17 to 28 October 1955. By the start of 1958 about 750 people had attended a total of 23 courses. Participants came from a wide variety of engineering and commercial organisations. It was estimated that 40 per cent of attendees subsequently became full-time or part-time programmers. (Photo courtesy of the Museum of Science and Industry in Manchester.)

increased to £35,000 on average. (Actually, each machine was quoted for individually because of different installation/configuration requirements, though there were never any favoured-customer differentials.) Towards the end of the production run for the first ten machines, a more careful analysis was again made of manufacturing costs, which showed that the losses on further orders at current prices could not be sustained. As a result, Manchester ruled that no further orders could be quoted for. This sales embargo lasted for nine months, and was later considered to have lost Ferranti anything up to 40 additional customers. The embargo certainly made life difficult for the marketing staff because, in the late 1950s, the lead-time between first contact of a customer to the placing of an order took at least one year, usually two, and sometimes three years.

In summary, the first price fixed, though not the first formally quoted, for Pegasus, was £32,000 including power supplies and the necessary paper-tape input/output equipment. The Pegasus 1 selling price without power supplies had risen to £42,000 by about October 1957. By the end of its selling life, the basic form of the more powerful Pegasus 2 was being quoted at £47,200 'delivered and erected'. At about the same time (1962), a four-bedroom terrace house in Manchester could be bought for £1200 and a four-door family saloon car typically cost about £700. (Specifically, the motoring extremes in 1962 were represented by an Austin Mini at £496 and a Rolls-Royce Silver Cloud II at £6272.)

4.2 What was Pegasus used for?

Although Pegasus was used successfully for a wide range of scientific and engineering applications, aircraft design predominated on 12 of the 40 computer installations listed in Section 4.4. Metal fatigue due to vibrational stresses had caused several aircraft disasters in the mid-1950s and it was realised that so-called flutter calculations were a vital part of aeroplane design. From the outset, Pegasus was supplied with library software containing the matrix interpretive scheme described in Chapter 3. Each instruction in this scheme specified one matrix operation, and it was therefore easy to program the sequence of matrix calculations required in aircraft design and similar engineering tasks.

The first Pegasus was installed at Ferranti's London Computer Centre at 21 Portland Place, where many customers made use of the standard application programs available there. For example, a set of frame-stressing programs was widely employed to analyse the stresses in large structures, such as buildings and flyovers, to ensure their safe design. The spectacular roof of the Sydney Opera House was one of many structures analysed on the Pegasus at Portland Place. The same Ferranti technical team provided a service for the analysis of stresses in pipe systems. Somewhat later, critical-path analysis for project planning became a major activity at Portland Place, and techniques for solving problems by successive approximations were evolved.

Amongst the early visitors to the centre writing their own programs was a team from the Post Office who used Pegasus to check the randomness of ERNIE, a special-purpose electronic machine which picked prize-winning premium bond numbers. (These bonds were, and still are, investment bonds administered by the UK's Department of National Savings.)

Other scientific applications included: operational research; turbine design; transformer design; optical lens design including aspherical surfaces; analysis of data from guided weapon trials, wind-tunnel experiments and engine tests; and mapping survey calculations. The twenty-fifth production Pegasus, the machine in the Science Museum's collections, was used at University College, London, to continue work started at the Ferranti London Computer Centre in 1956, for the analysis of crystal structures from data measured on X-ray diffraction images.

Machine	Date first delivered	Number delivered to UK by July 1956	Additional exports by 1956
Ferranti Mark I	1951	1	1 (Canada)
LEO I★	1951	1	–
Ferranti Mark I Star	1953	4	2 (Holland, Italy)
Elliott 401★	1953	1	–
HEC/BTM 1200	1953	4	–
Deuce	1955	2	–
Deuce Mark 1	1955	4	–
Deuce Mark 2	1955	1	–
Elliott 402	1955	2	1 (France)
Elliott 403	1955	–	1 (Australia)
Elliott 405	1956	1	–
BTM/ICT 1201	1956	2	–

★ Note: LEO I and the Elliott 401 were both one-off machines.

Turning to more general applications and commercial data processing, Pegasus computers were used for road accident statistics, production control, railway timetables, stock control, payroll administration and current account book-keeping.

Many of the above tasks broke new ground, often initiated by programming effort at Ferranti's London Computer Centre. Through all these applications, Pegasus systems contributed significantly to the wider adoption of the digital computer as a useful design tool.

4.3 Competitors in the market place

When Pegasus was first demonstrated to prospective customers in 1956, the use of stored-program computers in the UK was confined to a few universities and a handful of large organisations. Existing applications were primarily in the field of science and engineering, with the commercial data processing market only beginning to be opened up.

By July 1956, shortly after the first Pegasus was completed in March of that year, 23 British-designed computers, of 12 types, are believed to have been in production and use in the UK (Table 4.1). It is thought that no computers of foreign manufacture were in use in the UK at that time; the first to reach Britain, an IBM 650, was installed in IBM's Data Processing Centre, London, in October 1956.

Figure 4.5 The tall cabinet to the centre right of this photograph is the Pegasus Converter, an add-on unit which enabled a company's existing punched-card data-processing equipment to be integrated with the magnetic tape system of a Pegasus 2 computer. The converter also offered off-line printing and card-conversion facilities. (Photo courtesy of Ferranti archive and ICL.)

Pegasus was first targeted at scientific and engineering applications. The main UK market competitors for Pegasus in 1956 were the English Electric Deuce and the Elliott 402 (Table 4.1). Of the other computers listed, the Ferranti Mark I and Mark I Star were about to be superseded by the Ferranti Mercury at the top end of the market. LEO I and the Elliott 401 were not really production machines. The Elliott 405 was just about to appear as a data-processing, rather than scientific, system, and the HEC/BTM offerings were small data-processing systems (see below). The approximate 1956 prices of Pegasus and its competitors were as follows: English Electric Deuce £42,000; Ferranti Pegasus £35,000; Elliott 402 £25,000. The Deuce had a faster raw computing speed than Pegasus (see Table 5.1, page 50), but required optimum programming techniques to sustain this advantage. As noted in Section 3.1, Pegasus claimed other advantages in ease of use and reliability. By the end of their production runs in the early 1960s, Pegasus had outsold its initial market competitors (see Table 5.2, page 55).

The entry labelled HEC/BTM 1200 in Table 4.1 deserves more explanation. A D Booth of Birkbeck College, University of London, had spent six months with von Neumann's computer group at Princeton University in 1947. He returned to England to design and implement several small-scale stored-program computers, culminating with the series called APE(X)C – All-purpose Electronic (X) Computers – where 'X' stood for the name of one of several project sponsors. By late 1950 the British Tabulating Machine Company had decided to construct 'a small low-cost semi-scientific computer' and, by mid-1951, had begun building a machine called HEC (Hollerith Electronic Computer) to Booth's specification. In early 1953 a HEC prototype, with a magnetic drum store, was demonstrated at the Business Efficiency Exhibition in London. The first production machine, HEC 2M, was delivered early in 1955; it contained some enhancements designed to suit commercial data-processing applications. The HEC series of machines were re-named the BTM 1200.

Within the same time frame as Table 4.1, large numbers of commercially-available computers had appeared in the USA (see Table 4.2). None of these US-manufactured machines is believed to have found its way to the UK by July 1956.

A performance comparison between Pegasus and several other computers, both earlier and later in time, is given in Section 5.1. However, whilst US computers are in mind, it is worth commenting upon the IBM Model 650,

Table 4.2 Some commercially-available US computers in the mid-1950s, with date of first delivery in the USA

Computer	First delivered
ERA 1101	1951
UNIVAC 1	1951
ERA 1102	1952
UNIVAC 1101	1952
NCR 102A	1952
ERA 1103	1953
IBM 701	1953
IBM 650	1954
UNIVAC 1102	1954
Burroughs E101	1954
NCR 102D	1954
Raytheon RAYDAC	1954
UNIVAC 1103	1955
IBM 704	1955
IBM 702/5	1955
RCA BIZMAC 1	1955
RCA BIZMAC 2	1956
NCR 303	1956
UNIVAC 2	1956

which sold in large numbers during the same period as Pegasus. The IBM 650 first arrived in the UK in October 1956 in the month that a Pegasus was first delivered to an external customer. Pegasus was felt by many to be, 'a much better computer than the IBM 650 at about the same price.' However, by the time the last of 40 Pegasus computers had been delivered in 1962, about 1800 IBM 650s had been sold worldwide. In terms of numbers sold, the IBM 650 out-performed all other contemporary machines by an order of magnitude. In the academic field, IBM was able to offer a 40 per cent discount to customers – which put computer companies such as Ferranti at a serious marketing disadvantage.

The IBM 650 was a decimal (biquinary) computer, aimed more at the business data processing market than Pegasus (which was more scientific). The 650 was a card-in, card-out machine that integrated smoothly with existing standard business procedures based on Hollerith-type electromechanical punched-card equipment.

The IBM 650 had a slower clock period of eight microseconds, compared with Pegasus' three microseconds, and had a drum for main memory (therefore lacking the Pegasus computing store or RAM; see Section 3.2). The 650 had a single accumulator, and a (1+1)-address instruction format which specified the location of the next instruction. This permitted optimum programming which, as was observed in Section 2.4, was one of the intellectually-challenging 'skills' that the designers of Pegasus wished to dispense with. The 650's storage capacity was either 1000 or 2000 words, each word being ten decimal digits. The drum had a comparatively very fast revolution time of 4.8 milliseconds. The transfer time for one word was 96 microseconds. The fixed-point addition time depended upon the time to access the instruction and its operand from the drum which, in turn, depended upon the drum's rotational position. In the best case, which the skilled programmer aimed for, the add time was 576 microseconds. The worst time was 9.984 milliseconds. In Table 5.1 in the next chapter we take an average time of 5.184 milliseconds.

An interesting feature of the 650's otherwise simple instruction set was a Table Lookup order, which could scan data at drum-revolution speed. In the course of its long life, several incremental enhancements were made to the IBM 650. These included index registers, floating-point hardware, and a 60-word fast working memory (using magnetic cores).

Table 4.3 Definitive list of all 40 Pegasus 1 and Pegasus 2 computers built

Serial no. and destination	Date delivered
1 Ferranti Ltd Computing Service, London; (later, to Vickers)	March 1956
2 Hawker Aircraft Ltd, Kingston-upon-Thames	Oct. 1956
3 Admiralty Research Laboratory, Teddington	Feb. 1957
4 Sir W G Armstrong Whitworth Aircraft Ltd, Coventry	Nov. 1956
5 Royal Aircraft Establishment, Farnborough, Hants	May 1957
6 Vickers-Armstrongs (Aircraft) Ltd, Weybridge; (later, to Manchester Museum of Science & Industry)	May 1957
7 ICI Dyestuffs Division, Manchester – (first Pegasus 1 with Hollerith punched cards)	Dec. 1957
8 NRDC, Northampton Polytechnic, London	June 1957
9 De Havilland Aircraft Co. Ltd, Hatfield	Aug. 1957
10 BTH (AEI), (Rugby) Ltd	Aug. 1957
11 BISRA, London	Nov. 1957
12 Leeds University	Oct. 1957
13 Durham University	Oct. 1957
14 Southampton University	March 1958
15 Babcock & Wilcox Ltd, London	Jan. 1958
16 The United Steel Companies Ltd, Sheffield	Jan. 1958
17 Blackburn Aircraft Ltd, Brough, Yorkshire	March 1958
18 Svenska Flygmotor AB, Trollhättan	June 1958
19 MOS, Military Survey, Feltham, Middlesex	Aug. 1959
20 Stuttgart University	June 1958
21 Ferranti Ltd, Hollinwood	Aug. 1959
22 London & Manchester Ass Co. Ltd, London (Known as Pluto, it had Powers punched card equipment)	Oct. 1960
23 CA Parsons & Co. Ltd, Newcastle	Jan. 1959
24 The Steel Co. of Wales Ltd, Port Talbot	Feb. 1960
25 Skandia, Sweden; Ferranti; UCL. 'Pegasus 1+'; operational, Science Museum.	Dec. 1959
26 Ferranti Ltd, Newman Street (Pegasus 2)	Aug. 1960
27 Ferranti-Packard Electric Ltd, Toronto (Pegasus 1)	Dec. 1959
28 Bruce Peebles & Co. Ltd, Edinburgh (Pegasus 2)	Oct. 1960
29 DSIR, Road Research Lab., Harmondsworth (Pegasus 2)	Jan. 1961
30 The College of Aeronautics, Cranfield, Beds (Pegasus 1)	Sept. 1960
31 Shell Refining Co. Ltd, Stanlow, Cheshire (Pegasus 2)	Feb. 1961
32 Shell Research Ltd, Thornton, Cheshire (Pegasus 2)	Feb. 1961
33 Vickers-Armstrongs (Aircraft) Ltd, Weybridge (Pegasus 2)	June 1961
34 De Havilland Aircraft Co. Ltd, Hatfield (Pegasus 2)	Sept. 1961
35 Martins Bank Ltd, Liverpool (Pegasus 2)	April 1961
36 The Edinburgh Computers Ltd, Edinburgh (formerly Scottish Widows fund and Standard Life Assurance Co.) (Pegasus 2)	April 1962
37 A & AEE, Boscombe Down, Wiltshire (Pegasus 1)	Jan. 1962
38 Westminster Bank Ltd, London (Pegasus 2)	Nov. 1961
39 National Provincial Bank Ltd, London (Pegasus 2)	May 1962
40 British Railways, Eastern Region (Pegasus 2)	Oct. 1962

4.4 List of the 40 Pegasus computers built (see Table 4.3)

It can be inferred from Table 4.3 that the Pegasus design permitted a series of enhancements. As described in Section 3.3, a Pegasus computer installation consists of a number of cabinets of equipment. The basic unit, or 'sub-cabinet', is the bay, a 71-cm-wide section clearly seen in the photograph in Figure 2.9. The original Pegasus 1 was referred to as a three-bay computer, but from its inception the design was intended to be extensible. The Skandia Pegasus, number 25 in Table 4.3 and on display at the Science Museum in London, is a four-bay machine. Several early Pegasus 1s were delivered with separate free-standing control units for magnetic tape and for punched cards or line printers. Pegasus number 22, designated Pluto, pioneered the fourth computer bay with additional fast store (intermediate access store) made up from 336-bit nickel delay lines; Pluto also had some additional instructions for more efficient handling of six-bit characters. These facilities were later included in the Skandia machine displayed in the Science Museum and subsequently in the new Pegasus 2 design.

The Skandia Pegasus originally had a separate card control unit adapted to drive punched-card readers and printers which were to be supplied in

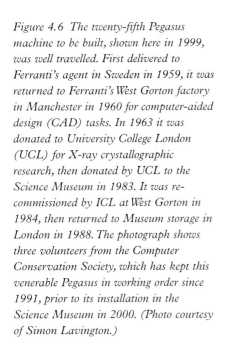

Figure 4.6 The twenty-fifth Pegasus machine to be built, shown here in 1999, was well travelled. First delivered to Ferranti's agent in Sweden in 1959, it was returned to Ferranti's West Gorton factory in Manchester in 1960 for computer-aided design (CAD) tasks. In 1963 it was donated to University College London (UCL) for X-ray crystallographic research, then donated by UCL to the Science Museum in 1983. It was re-commissioned by ICL at West Gorton in 1984, then returned to Museum storage in London in 1988. The photograph shows three volunteers from the Computer Conservation Society, which has kept this venerable Pegasus in working order since 1991, prior to its installation in the Science Museum in 2000. (Photo courtesy of Simon Lavington.)

Sweden by Ferranti's agent, LM Ericssons Driftkontrol AB. In the event the specifications of the card equipment and the control unit did not meet the customer's needs and the machine was eventually returned to Manchester where Ferranti used it for systems development. In November 1963 the machine was donated to University College London (UCL), where it was used for crystallographic research until 1980 (see Figure 4.6).

The sixth Pegasus, shown in Figure 1.1 and Figure 4.7, was donated to Brooklands Technical College after its useful life at Vickers. This computer was then acquired in 1969 by the Museum of Science & Industry in Manchester, where it is now on display but not in working order.

Figure 4.7 The computer room at the British Aircraft Corporation's Weybridge factory in about 1965. This factory, formerly Vickers-Armstrong (Aircraft) Ltd, took delivery of a Pegasus 1 in May 1957, a Pegasus 2 in June 1961 and then the original Portland Place Pegasus some time after mid-1963. All three machines can be seen in this photograph. They were used for stress calculations, wind-tunnel modelling, general aircraft design work, and for preparing sales promotional material. By the end of the 1960s, these Pegasus machines had been replaced by ICL1900 series computers. (Photo courtesy of Mrs J C Matthews.)

5 Pegasus' place in history

5.1 Comparative performance

We may get some idea of how the raw performance of Pegasus compared with its contemporaries, and incidentally with modern PCs, by calculating the speed and main memory capacity of a selection of computers (see Table 5.1).

Obtaining figures for 'speed' is not an exact science, because a given computer may appear relatively faster or slower than another computer, depending upon the nature of the particular benchmark program being executed. A rough measure of speed, often used, is the number of simple instructions that can be executed per second, where a 'simple instruction' could be a fixed-point Add. Even this measure is subject to some debate in the case of computers that allow optimum programming, as was discussed for the case of the IBM 650 in Section 4.3. The English Electric Deuce in Table 5.1 is another computer for which optimum programming techniques were necessary to get the best performance. Deuce's best add-time was 64 microseconds, but a more typical figure within a general programming context might be about 128 microseconds.

From Table 5.1 it is clear that Pegasus would have been classed as a medium-range computer in the mid-1950s. Thirty years later, by which time the personal computer and semiconductor technology had really begun to have an impact on society at large, the Pegasus performance would have seemed extremely slow. One benchmark test, a program to detect prime numbers by the method of Eratosthenes' sieve, showed that a modest 50 MHz 486 PC with 20 Mbytes of RAM was about 50,000 times faster than Pegasus when finding all the primes up to 16,384. However, during this benchmark program, Pegasus had to spend much time packing and unpacking data because of its small memory. A comparison of simple loops of instructions suggests that the same PC was only about 3000 times faster than Pegasus in terms of raw computing speed.

We choose the Cambridge University EDSAC as the baseline in Table 5.1 because EDSAC was the first fully-functional stored-program computer in the world to run a regular service to users. It also happens that the two performance measures chosen for comparative purposes are close to unity for EDSAC, thus making possible such awe-inspiring but vague statements as 'the machine on my desk is half a million times more powerful than the

Table 5.1 Comparing the computing speed and memory capacity of certain representative computers.

Computer	Year delivered	CPU speed, KIPS	On-line storage, kbytes
Cambridge EDSAC	1949	0.7	2
Ferranti Mark I Star	1953	0.8	82
IBM 650	1954	0.2	40
English Electric Deuce	1955	8	34
IBM 704	1955	42	162
BTM/ICT 1201	1956	8	20
Ferranti Pegasus	1956	3	25
Ferranti Mercury	1957	17	165
Ferranti Atlas	1962	621	768
Intel 8086 PC	1978	330	8
Intel 80486 PC	1989	20,000	5120
Intel P3/400 PC	1999	400,000	4,161,000

Notes.

a) Speed is expressed as the number of kilo-instructions per second, so that conversion can easily be made to the modern measure of MIPS (millions of instructions per second). In this context, an 'instruction' is taken as a fixed-point Add.

b) On-line storage is taken as the sum of random-access memory (e.g. CRT, short delay lines, core or semiconductor) and sequential memory (e.g. long delay lines, drum or hard disk), where information can be swapped between RAM and secondary storage under program control.

c) The following assumptions have been made about configuration options. IBM 704: assume 4096 words of core, and four drums (each 8 k words). ICT 1201: assume a 4080-word drum. Mercury: assume four drums. Atlas: assume 192 kbytes of core. Intel-based PCs: assume typical 8086, 80486 and the Pentium P3 machines would have had respectively none, 4 Mbytes, and 4 Gbytes of hard disk.

first Cambridge computer.' One of the reasons such statements are 'vague' is that they take no account of ease of programming. Since ease of programming was one of the design objectives of Pegasus, we should now try to assess the degree to which Pegasus was innovative.

5.2 Architectural innovations

Raw computing power is of little use unless it is readily accessible to the programmer. We make a distinction between 'programmer' and 'user', because it is the former who has to provide the system software (assemblers, compilers, operating systems, libraries, utilities, database management systems, word-processing packages, etc.) which turns a piece of passive electronic equipment into a useful problem-solving tool.

The factors that make one computer more programmer-friendly than another need to be set in the context of what was technically and economically possible at the time. By 1954/55, when the Pegasus design got under way, there was agreement by the pioneers of computing that the following were amongst the desirable attributes of an instruction set architecture for a general-purpose computer:

a) word length of at least 32 bits;

b) hardware facilities for indexing (address-modification);

c) fixed-point multiply instruction.

Although Pegasus, in common with many of its contemporaries in Table 5.1, had these attributes, it is interesting to recall that it was not economically possible for the first generation of single-chip microprocessors to have attributes (a) and (c) in the 1970s.

By the mid-1960s, experts agreed that the following additional attributes were desirable:

d) floating-point hardware instructions;

e) hardware for memory management in two-level stores, for example virtual-to-real address translation hardware.

In Table 5.1 the IBM 704 was the first production computer to incorporate attribute (d). In a very modest sense, Pegasus went some way towards (e) with its facilities for block indexing/counting. However, referring to Table 5.1, the Ferranti Atlas was the first computer to possess both attributes (d) and (e). Single-chip microcomputers did not catch up until the late 1980s. By the 1990s, the demand for high-speed, high-resolution graphics had made floating-point facilities important in commodity computers.

In the context of the mid-1950s, attributes (a) to (d) might be seen as the natural outcomes of computing experience to that date. Compared with these, the symmetrical instruction set of Pegasus, with its group of eight accumulators/index registers, was mould-breaking. It is perhaps the most important architectural innovation to emerge from Christopher Strachey's design. It had a strong influence on the instruction set of most subsequent

Figure 5.1 A rear view of the cabinets of a Ferranti Perseus computer (see also Figure 5.2). This arrangement of so-called back wiring was typical of the physical layout of computers in the early 1960s. (Photo courtesy of Ferranti archive and ICL.)

Ferranti computers such as the Sirius, Perseus, Orion, Argus, the FP6000 project and hence on the ICT/ICL 1900 series. The first computer in the ICT 1900 range was delivered to a customer in January 1965. By 1968, over a thousand ICL 1900 series machines had been installed.

In the period 1956–66 the notion of a general register set, introduced in Pegasus, also began to have a significant influence on US computer design. In their seminal book *Computer Structures: Readings and Examples*, Professors Gordon Bell and Allen Newell comment thus: 'Pegasus is, we think, about the earliest computer to use general registers.' When analysing various candidate architectures in terms of the instruction-set processor (ISP) notation, Bell and Newell comment that, 'Pegasus has the nicest ISP processor structure discussed in this section – perhaps in this book... It is probably the first machine to use an array of general registers as accumulators, multiplier-quotient registers, index registers, etc.' The first US-designed computer to adopt the general register organisation was the UNIVAC 1107 (delivered in 1962). The CDC6600 (delivered in 1963) is a variant because it had three sets of general registers. The IBM 360 series (first delivered in 1964) also used a general register organisation but had a weaker (less symmetrical) implementation. The SDS Sigma 5 (delivered in 1967) adopted the general-register organisation, as did increasing numbers of computer designers during the 1970s until, by 1980, the general-register notion had become the *de facto* starting point for practically all processor designs worldwide. An exception is the zero-address (or stack) family of computers, of which early examples were the English Electric KDF9 and the Burroughs B5000, both first delivered in 1963.

Thus, if one had to pick one innovative highlight of the Pegasus architecture, it would be the notion of a general register set.

Returning to Ferranti, the Manchester-based designers of Atlas did not follow the Pegasus idea of general registers and a single arithmetic unit. Being more interested in high performance, they expanded the philosophy, first seen in the Manchester University Mark I, of having separate registers and processing hardware for (a) computation, and (b) housekeeping. 'Housekeeping' in this context means address-generation, counting, indexing, memory management, etc. This notion of separate functional sub-units was costly but allowed a higher degree of concurrent operation and simplified the pipeline design. The first Atlas computer was operational by December 1962 (see below). The concept of separate functional units and explicit hardware facilities for housekeeping found favour in the ICL 2980, first delivered in June 1975 and strongly influenced by a Manchester University prototype known as MU5. By the late 1990s, the idea of separate, concurrent, functional units was influencing the design of commodity microprocessors – which also usually combined their functional sub-units with the Pegasus notion of general registers. Semiconductor technology had by then reached the point where all the registers and functional sub-units could be fabricated on a single silicon chip.

5.3 What happened next? The UK computer industry in the 1960s

As seen from Table 4.3, the last Pegasus computer to be sold was delivered to British Railways, Eastern region, in October 1962. The original Pegasus engineering team had largely dispersed; for example Bill Elliott, Charles Owen, Ian Merry and Harry Metcalfe all moved to IBM in the autumn of 1956. Meanwhile, the other Ferranti design engineers had not been idle. By the end of the 1950s four new Ferranti computer projects were in progress: Perseus, Sirius, Orion and Atlas. The first two owed much to Pegasus.

Perseus was a large data-processing computer, targeted at insurance companies (see Figure 5.2). In hardware terms, it used Pegasus packages – a testimony to the robustness and flexibility of the original circuit design. Perseus had a 72-bit word length, a word representing either 12 six-bit characters or three 24-bit instructions. Perseus worked directly on alpha-numeric characters and could perform mixed-radix arithmetic (e.g. for pounds, shillings and pence). In other respects, the instruction set, totalling 63 operations, was based on Pegasus. Addition took 234 microseconds. The computing store consisted of nickel delay lines, arranged as 32 blocks of 32 words each. Actually, this memory was in three parts: 32 registers in single-word lines; four blocks of 32 words in single-word lines; 27 blocks of 32 words held in 16-word long lines. Hence, the first two parts were random-access. The Perseus main store consisted of 16 magnetic tape decks. Input was via paper tape and cards (Powers-Samas equipment); output was via an offline high-speed printer. The central processor contained much error-detecting hardware.

The second Ferranti computer to derive its instruction set from Pegasus was the Sirius. This was a decimal machine, where each word represented ten decimal digits. The store consisted of long (torsional) nickel delay lines. However, the logic circuits departed completely from the Pegasus packages. Instead, they were based on novel forms of transistor-ferrite core logic circuit called neurons by their inventor, Gordon Scarrott. Sirius was a modest,

Figure 5.2 A Ferranti Perseus computer, shown at Ferranti's Lily Hill House premises at Bracknell, to the west of London. Perseus, which used the same packaged circuits as Pegasus, was the first Ferranti computer to be designed specifically to meet the needs of large commercial data-processing organisations. Only two Perseus machines were delivered: to insurance companies in Stockholm and Cape Town, respectively in April and December of 1959. Some Ferranti marketing staff felt that sales were inhibited by the internal politics of links between Ferranti and the punched-card equipment manufacturer Powers-Samas. (Photo courtesy of Ferranti archive and ICL.)

general-purpose machine which, at £20,000, was advertised as 'the smallest and most economically-priced computer in Europe'. Twenty Sirius machines were delivered between December 1961 and March 1963.

By June 1962, the penetration of the UK market by foreign companies was running at about 18 per cent of a total of approximately 475 installed machines. A league table of the dozen most popular computers is given in Table 5.2.

While the installed base of home-produced small-to-medium computers was growing rapidly in the UK, Britain had seriously fallen behind the USA in the design of large, powerful computers. This was confirmed in a report dated May 1956 to the Department of Scientific & Industrial Research (DSIR) Advisory Committee on High Speed Calculating Machines (the Brunt Committee). In April 1956, Brian Pollard (Ferranti) told a computer design conference that, 'There is in this country a range of medium-speed computers, and the only two machines which are really fast are the Cambridge EDSAC 2 and the University of Manchester Mark 2, although both are still very slow compared with the fastest American machines.

Table 5.2 The 12 most popular makes of computer in the UK in 1962, as measured by the total installed base as at June 1962. The impression given by the entries should be treated with caution because Table 5.2 is a mix of small- and medium-sized machines, as may be judged by the performance figures given previously in Table 5.1. Furthermore, Table 5.2 does not include large computers such as the IBM 7090, of which four had been installed in the UK by June 1962.

Manufacturer/model	Origin	Date first delivered in UK	No. delivered to UK by June 1962
NCR/Elliott 803	UK*	1960	53
Ferranti Pegasus 1 & 2	UK	1956	37 (+3 exported)
IBM 1401	USA	1960	34
ICT 1201	UK	1956	29 (+9 exported)
English Electric Deuce 1,2,2A	UK	1955	28 (+2 exported)
NCR/Elliott 405	UK	1956	27 (+4 exported)
STC Stantec Zebra	UK/NL**	1958	16 (+23 'exported')
ICT 1202	UK	1959	16 (+5 exported)
Ferranti Mercury	UK	1957	14 (+5 exported)
EMI Emidec 1100	UK	1959	13 (+1 exported)
IBM 650	USA	1956	13
Ferranti Sirius	UK	1961	12 (+4 exported)

Notes

* The first 803 was delivered in the USA in Nov. 1959. The next five went to the USA; then: Germany, USA, Russia, Germany, then the first UK installation (Sheffield) in July 1960. Elliott Brothers did not get one until Dec. 1960.

** The Stantec Zebra was designed by W L van der Poel of the Dutch Postal and Telecommunications Services and manufactured by Standard Telephones & Cables Ltd., England. The first eight machines went to: Holland, Switzerland, Holland, UK, Holland (3), UK.

We ought to be a little worried that no serious effort is being made to produce at least one really large fast machine.'

By 1959 Ferranti Ltd had embarked upon the design and production of two large computer projects. The first was a joint venture with the University of Manchester, encouraged by a loan from NRDC. This project, led by Tom Kilburn of Manchester University, produced the Atlas computer. Atlas was officially unveiled to the press on 7 December 1962 and was running a scientific computing service from January 1963. For a brief period of history, Atlas was considered to be the most powerful computer in the world, the Ferranti salesmen equating it to four IBM 7094s. Perhaps of more lasting significance, Atlas introduced the idea of virtual memory. Concurrent with the Atlas activity, Ferranti was developing the Orion computer – another large machine, whose sales prospects were directed more towards the business data-processing market. In its early stages the Orion project was beset with technical difficulties concerning the robustness of its neuron logic circuits. By 1963 deliveries of Atlas and Orion computers had begun, but sales were slow in coming. In the event, Ferranti sold three large Atlas installations, and three reduced-facility installations including the interesting Titan variant developed at Cambridge University. A total of 14 Orion 1 and Orion 2 machines were built.

If the marketing of large computers to the scientific community was causing problems for UK manufacturers, so was the marketing of small and medium machines to the business community. We saw in Chapter 4 how Ferranti had sought liaisons with the punched-card equipment suppliers. Similarly, by 1957 Elliott Brothers had linked up with the UK wing of the US company NCR (National Cash Register) to market the Elliott 405 computer. It is estimated that the sales of Elliott/NCR computers during the period 1950–59 amounted to about 32 per cent of the total UK market by value, while Ferranti's share was about 26 per cent of the computer market by value. However, the profits in real terms were not sufficient to sustain either company in the long term.

In September 1963 Ferranti Ltd sold its mainframe computer business to International Computers and Tabulators (ICT). ICT had been formed in 1959 by the merger of the UK's two main punched-card equipment companies: Powers-Samas and BTM. There then followed a series of mergers amongst the main UK computer manufacturers. The result was the company International Computers Ltd (ICL) which, by 1968, embraced the computer-related components of such UK firms as BTM, Powers-Samas, ICT, Ferranti, GEC, EMI, English Electric, Leo, Marconi and Elliott Brothers. All this is well documented in Martin Campbell-Kelly's book *ICL: a Business and Technical History*. Both the Borehamwood and the Portland Place legacies therefore survived, in some small degree, within the culture of the UK's indigenous computer industry.

5.4 In conclusion

Summarising the Pegasus legacy, in the beginning the UK's National Research Development Corporation had the vision of a medium-priced, packaged computer. Resulting NRDC contracts led to the 401 machine, which helped to bring the Borehamwood defence electronic know-how into the civil arena and propel Elliott Brothers Ltd into the computer business. NRDC follow-on support for the FPC/1 and Pegasus projects helped to broaden Ferranti's approach to the computer market and, in the instruction

Figure 5.3 Charles Owen (1918–84). Graduating in 1941, Owen was drafted to an electronics company to work on air-to-air radar. After the war he joined Elliott Brothers at Borehamwood to work on the design of modular, packaged, electronic circuits for naval gunnery-control computers. His circuit expertise contributed significantly to the design of the Nicholas and 401 computers. He moved to Ferranti in 1954, to become a principal member of the Pegasus team. In 1956 he joined IBM to help found their UK laboratories at Hursley, near Winchester. He was involved with the design of the IBM System 360 computers and, in 1969, was honoured with a prestigious IBM Fellowship. (Photo courtesy of Ian Merry.)

set of Pegasus, left a lasting imprint on the design of subsequent Ferranti and ICL computers.

Lest this seem too much like a eulogy for NRDC, it has been said that NRDC often viewed the task of fostering a lively UK computer industry as 'like pushing mules uphill'. In turn, some industrialists in the 1950s viewed NRDC as a potential vehicle for government support for R&D and compared the relatively small NRDC seedcorn budget with the lavish US government sponsorship of the US computer companies. However, making such a comparison showed a misunderstanding of the original purpose for which NRDC was set up in 1949. The wider issue of appropriate UK government support for an indigenous computer industry in the 1950s and 1960s is another subject altogether.

Back to Pegasus. This has primarily been a story about engineering, in both the hardware and software senses of that word. It was a team effort, during which 35 or more people contributed their skills and enthusiasm over a period of about five years. Although it is difficult to list all the Pegasus players and their contributions, we should highlight the following individuals for special mention:

Bill Elliott as team-builder and external negotiator;
George Felton as software systems designer and implementer;
Charles Owen (Figure 5.3) as circuit designer and systems architect;
Christopher Strachey as logical designer and instruction-set originator.

Brian Maudsley oversaw the thorough mechanical design and Ian Merry developed the high-performance drum store. The engineering project did not, of course, exist in isolation. Credit should go to Lord Halsbury and John Crawley of NRDC for the initial enthusiasm and enabling contracts, and to Bernard Swann for understanding the value of Pegasus and how to sell it.

While the total sales fell short of expectations, Pegasus set new standards for reliability and ease of use in the 1950s. In the wider historical context, Martin Campbell-Kelly, when reviewing the development of programming in Britain during the period 1945–55, has said that Pegasus, 'opened up a new era in the provision of high-quality programming systems by manufacturers of computers in Britain ... it marks a turning-point from a situation of laissez-faire to one of strong involvement.' On the international stage, the huge number of modern commodity computers with a general register-set architecture is testimony to the usefulness of Christopher Strachey's ideas for Pegasus.

Index